NAMING
ARKANSAS

NAMING ARKANSAS

Curious Place Names from Greasy Corner to Sock City

DANIEL BOICE

THE
History
PRESS

Published by The History Press
Charleston, SC
www.historypress.com

Front cover: Aerial view of the University of Arkansas central campus. *Courtesy of University Relations, University of Arkansas.*

First published 2024

Manufactured in the United States

ISBN 9781467155632

Library of Congress Control Number: 2023947109

CONTENTS

ACKNOWLEDGEMENTS

Many puzzled Arkansans have politely repeated their town's name on being quizzed by the oddly curious librarian, and I appreciate their patience with me. The University of Arkansas at Monticello provided me with space and equipment for my work, and Teresa Bostian obtained many books via interlibrary loan. Public service staff at the Butler Center for Arkansas Studies and the Arkansas State Archives provided gracious assistance. Dr. Guy Lancaster, editor of the magisterial *Encyclopedia of Arkansas*, encouraged my project and graciously offered insightful suggestions for helping my work see the light of day. Chad Rhoad and Zoe Ames at The History Press have been unfailingly helpful. And my brilliant wife, Dr. Shari Silzell, has listened to more tales of place names with more informed kindness than any scribbler has a right to hope for.

INTRODUCTION

If, as Samuel Johnson said, "The chief glory of every people arises from its authors," then perhaps the most interesting glories of a state are its place names. Some Arkansas place names, like the Simpsons' mythical Springfield, are shared with other states, but many names are unique. Arkansas is blessed by a wonderful variety of interesting place names, often with delightful stories of their origins and pronunciations that can baffle all but natives.

Celebrating that plethora of names, stories and pronunciations is the purpose of this book, which started out as a simple aid for the author in his travels and evolved into an ever-growing project. The result is an all-too-abbreviated amalgam of some Arkansas place names that might be useful to travelers from other states, as well as to Arkansans in their own journeys.

This book gathers place names from centuries of exploration and settlement, of recognizing local features and of celebrating local uniqueness, including the pronunciation of names when those pronunciations might not otherwise be obvious. For space considerations, this listing includes (almost) only place names whose origins are known or at least guessed at. Many—too many!—places are not listed here but should be. There are many wonderful place names whose stories deserve to be told, and maybe this book will help uncover some of them.

A few scholars of language have provided insightful essays about some of the currents that have guided the formation and pronunciation of Arkansas place names. Newspaper historian Fred Allsopp gathered a number of stories, but no one was more curious about or more delighted by the glory of Arkansas names than journalist Ernie Deane, whose book *Arkansas Place Names* forms a solid basis for this and all such future guides.

Each entry notes the county where the place is located and, occasionally, the place name's pronunciation, in italics. Space limitations regrettably led to the exclusion of the names of many towns, especially those no longer existent and, also, too many whose names came from early settlers. Modern communities, whose names were coined in order to sell property, as well as lakes and dams named for political or corporate sponsors are mostly left out, also. Finally, the names of most counties have obvious sources or can be easily located elsewhere.

I have made errors aplenty herein. Some of my tales are guesswork, and there are many tales yet untold. Many pronunciations will need refining. Readers who can correct and enlighten the author on either count will be appreciated and their corrections welcomed. Because such an undertaking, with new towns springing up and new generations finding new ways to say old names, will never be finished—and that, too, is a cause to celebrate.

Join me in this celebration!

Chapter 1

INDIGENOUS, FRENCH
AND EARLY SETTLERS

P rior to the arrival of White settlers in what is now Arkansas, the Indigenous peoples had few permanent settlements. Hunting caches along rivers were used seasonally, and mounds still stand to show where Indians centered their encampments. Spanish conquistadors and French missionaries recorded a few place names, but their descriptions and hasty cartographic sketches have frustrated most attempts to locate the villages. As the press of Indian tribes moving ahead of the inexorable White expansion led to the departures of the Caddo and the Quapaw, their place names vanished with them. Only a few echoes of Indigenous words are still heard in Arkansas place names.

The first Europeans to put down stakes—literally—in Arkansas were Spanish explorers who did not tarry. Later, French missionaries arrived at about the same time as hunters and trappers, and a number of natural features, especially streams and especially in the southern half of the state, still bear French names, albeit often with spellings and pronunciations considerably changed.

As the new American nation was slowly growing to the West—a process that gathered momentum with the Louisiana Purchase—a number of obstacles confronted prospective settlers. The western bank of the Mississippi, itself wide, fast and dangerous, was essentially a dense hedge of forest that grew thickly on the rich effluvial soil. In that flat land lurked the dangers of yellow fever and malaria, which regularly afflicted those hardy souls who tried to clear farmland. Beyond the Delta were hills—or "mountains," as the settlers called them—with steep sides, rocks aplenty and thin soil, so that existence was hardscrabble and settlements usually too tenuous for a name. Only gradually, as the rivers became traveled and some of the forests were cleared, did actual towns take root, and these were named primarily for the earliest settlers or for their hometowns whence they had come seeking a better life.

L'Aigle *LAY-gull* (creek in Bradley): The D'Aigle family in Arkansas Post was perhaps the source of this name.

Alabam *al-uh-BAM* (Madison): Probably named by settlers from Alabama.

L'Anguille River *lan-GEEL*: River on the western side of Crowley's Ridge, named in the eighteenth century by French trappers for the eels they caught there. Also called the West River in the early nineteenth century.

Arkansas *AR-kann-saw*: So called after a prominent Native American group, the Quapaw. Neighboring Algonquian speakers called the group the Akansa and so identified them to French missionaries. The French used that name and added an *s* to make the plural, although that *s* was not pronounced. Eventually, English-speaking settlers also came to use that term for the Quapaws and, eventually, call the entire territory by that word. But how to pronounce this word was a problem from the start. Some early settlers pronounced "Arkansas" to sound like the territory to the northwest (which was named for a different tribe, the Kansa) and said *ar-KAN-zuss*, while others said *AR-kan-saw*, with stubborn partisans on each side. The matter was finally settled by the state legislature in 1881.

Atlanta (Columbia): The area was settled by migrants from Georgia around 1850, and the town was named for the new city in that state.

Bard Springs (Polk): A local legend concerns an "Old Man Bard" who found the spring in 1802.

Bayou Bartholomew: A stream beginning near Pine Bluff and continuing for more than 350 miles southward, eventually flowing into the Ouachita River in Louisiana. It was perhaps named for an early French explorer nicknamed Little Bartholomew the Parisian, but there is also mention of a Louis Barthelmy, a Quapaw-French hunter.

Bayou de Loutre (Union): French (modified) for "Otter Bayou."

Bayou Lafriet (Clark): Some say that this appears as L'Eau Frais (*which see*) Creek on early state maps; it is sometimes called Low Freight Creek by area residents.

Bayou Meto *BYE-oh MEE-tuh*: A stream beginning in Pulaski County and meandering 150 miles into the Arkansas River near Gillett. It is labeled in some early French documents as Bayou Metre. Some speculate that it was one meter deep, while others suggest the name is from French *mi-terre*, "minor land," or *metaux*, "metals," on account of nearby mines. Until the spelling finally settled in the twentieth century, it was also spelled Bayou Metoe. Deane says that *mi-terre* means "halfway," because it was between the Arkansas and Mississippi Rivers.

Bellaire (Chicot): While "belle aire" is obviously French, for "nice air," one humorous local story says that the land once belonged to a farmer named Bell and, after his death, to his sons and so came to be known as the "Bell Heir" property.

Bismarck (Hot Spring): The settlement was first, if unimaginatively, called Cross Roads. The town's first letter carrier, Frank Holstein, perhaps German and a fan of the Prussian leader, got the first post office in 1883 named Bismarck.

Black Fork town and mountain (Scott): Both named for the Black Fork Creek, which was so named for its murky water.

Bodcaw town (Nevada) and creek (Lafayette): Named Bodka by an explorer among the Caddo Indians. An 1824 map identifies a Bodcau Creek, which in Arkansas is now Bodcaw Creek, while Louisiana preserves the earlier spelling. There is speculation that the name derives from the Choctaw word *bokko*, "a small hill," or is a misreading of the French name Bodeau or Badeau. A small settlement grew up in the middle of the nineteenth century, but only in the 1880s, with the coming of a lumber company named for the creek, did the town take its name.

Cache River: One story says that the river was named using the verb "to hunt" in the Picardie dialect used by some French hunters. Allsopp says it was originally called the Faux Cache, having to do with a "false or hidden" river.

Caddo River: Flows from Polk County into the Ouachita and is named for the Caddo Indians who lived in this area. *Caddo* is an abbreviation of *Cadohadacho*, which is now used to identify all Caddo people. That tribal name comes from *kade*, meaning "leader" or "principal chief," and until well into the 1800s, the river was still called Fourche des Cadaux.

Caddo Gap (Montgomery): Settled in the first half of the nineteenth century on the Caddo River but called Centreville until after the Civil War, when it got its more descriptive name.

Cadron Settlement Park (Faulkner): *Cadron* is French for "sundial," which would be an odd name for a town. Deane argues that Cadron is probably derived from the French *quadrant*, and he cites Thomas Nuttall's account of visiting a site called Cadron or Quadrant, which Nuttall interpreted as some sort of measurement. Dickinson thinks it "more likely that the name is a misspelling of another French *cadron*, a shortening of *cadronure*, 'star shape,' perhaps from a tree trunk," which makes even less sense than a sundial.

Camden: The seat of Ouachita County, established in the eighteenth century as a French trading post called Ecore a Fabri or Fabri's Bluff and later spelled Fabre. Deane notes that there is no evidence of a resident named Fabre and that some attribute the name to a New Orleans notary, Andry Farbry de la Bruyere, who explored the region. The name was changed when Ouachita County was formed in 1829 at the suggestion of one of the commissioners, General Thomas Woodward, who came from either Camden, South Carolina, or Camden, Alabama.

Carlisle (Lonoke): Samuel McCormick and his wife, L.J., settled here around 1872 and named the town, according to one story, for Carlisle, Pennsylvania, where they had once lived. Another, less likely story says that they named it in honor of a friend who was a senator in an unidentified state.

Casa Massa, creek in Clark County: A Civil War map shows Cache Masso post office, and a reasonable guess is that a French trapper named Macon at one time had a large cache there. Also spelled Cachamassa and Cassamassa.

Cerro Gordo or **Cerrogordo** (Little River): The site of a salt mine in the eighteenth century and near well-known salt licks on the Little River, the town was settled after the Civil War and notorious as a lawless place. It was named for the 1847 battle in the Mexican War.

Chickalah *shi-KEE-luh:* The town, creek and mountain in Yell County are all named for a legendary Chikileh or Chil-kil-leh, a Cherokee leader in the area around 1800, perhaps buried there. The town was established around 1830, and Chikileh's story was written by missionary Cephas Washburn, founder of the Dwight Mission near Russellville.

Chicot *SHEE-coh*, lake and county: The county took its name from the oxbow lake, which may have been named for Point Chicot, a stop on the Mississippi River. In 1795, Don Carlos De Villemont, a commander from Arkansas Post, received a grant of land for "Island del Chicot." There is evidence of a settlement in the early nineteenth century called Illechecko, which may be from the French Isle Chicot, "Island of Stumps" or "Stumpy Ground." Deane notes an Indian village, discovered by de Soto, called Chisca, as another possible source.

Chocktaw (Van Buren): Established before 1880, the town as well as Choctaw Creek were named for a nearby Choctaw camp.

Clarendon: The seat of Monroe County, established where the road from Memphis to Little Rock crossed the White River. Early on, it was called Mouth of the Cache, then Rockroe or Roe Rock. Deane says it was named for the Earl of Clarendon but doesn't explain why.

Columbia, a county and also a town in Randolph County: The county was apparently, like many cities in the United States, named for the female personification of America, who herself was named for Christopher Columbus. The town, a busy port on the Mississippi, was called by the French Fourche de Thomas, since it was on the Fourche Creek. It was the seat of Chicot County, from 1833 to 1855, but it was finally washed away in the 1880s.

Commissary (Greene): One story says this town was named for an 1861 Confederate supply depot. Another, equally likely, says that it commemorates Richard Jackson's Commissary, which served nearby lumber camps.

Cornerville (Lincoln): There are two stories about this small town's name. The most likely says that the town was named for the Tennessee hometown of founder Elias King Haynes. The weaker tale says that the name was given because the town was on the corner of four counties, even though there are only three nearby.

Cossatot River *KAHS-uh-taht*: Flows from around Mena to the Little River. A story says that the name came from an Indian word meaning "skull crusher," but the name is French, Cassetête, meaning "crushed head" or "brain teaser," perhaps owing to the dangerous rapids. More likely, as Deane notes, *cassetete* was the word for "tomahawk." Nuttall in 1819 records a Cassetete Mountain, later called Short Mountain.

Cusotte Bayou (Jefferson and Lincoln Counties): Probably named for Francisco Cousot, a member of the militia at Arkansas Post in 1780.

Debastrop Township (Ashley): Part of the grant given to Felipe Enrique Neri, Baron de Bastrop, in 1796. Arkansas kept the "de" that was cut from the Louisiana city's name.

Deceiper Creek *dee-SEE-per* (Clark): From the French Bayu de Cyper or Bayou de Cypres: i.e., Cypress Bayou.

Dover (Pope): Settled in the 1830s, with two possible names and three possible origins: perhaps Dr. Joseph Brearley named it for his hometown in Delaware or for the English city his family hailed from, or perhaps Stephen Rye named it for his hometown in Tennessee.

Dubuque (Boone): Settled in the early nineteenth century at a crossing of the White River and first called Sugarloaf Prairie. In the 1850s, the captain of the steamboat *Eureka* happened to dock there and suggested the name of his Iowa hometown, which became official in 1854. The town was destroyed in the Civil War, and the site is now beneath Bull Shoals Lake. It was eventually succeeded by Sugarloaf and then Diamond City.

L'Eau Frais Creek *Low Fray* (Clark): French for "cool water." Old maps show it as Lofreight, Low Freight and L'Eau Froide.

Elgin (Jackson): Settled in the first half of the nineteenth century at a ferry crossing of the White River, on a farm named for the Scottish home of the father of farmer Robert T. Dunbar.

Fourche LaFave River *FOOSH la-FAVE*: *Fourche* is French for "fork," and Pierre LeFevre, who was at Arkansas Post in 1791, probably gave his name to the river, which rises in the Ouachita Mountains and flows into the Arkansas River. The shortened form of that name is now used for a small settlement along its bank. The Fourche River in northeastern Arkansas empties into the Black River near Pocahontas. Fourche Creek lies mostly in the city limits of Little Rock and empties into the Arkansas River.

Fourche a Loupe Creek: *FOOSH-loop* or *FOOSH-ah-loo-PAY* (Garland and Hot Spring Counties): French for Wolf Fork Creek.

Frenchman's Bayou (Mississippi): This small community preserves a bit of French influence in the delta. Around 1628, says the story, LaSalle built a fort named Prudhomme for one of his men. Such a name was too difficult for later Arkansans, who, two centuries later, changed it.

Galla (or **Galley**) **Rock** and **Creek**, town, bluff and wildlife area (Pope and Yell Counties): One tale says that explorers in 1819 encountered a Cherokee village called Galley, but this is more than unlikely. More probably, the two-mile-long shale bluff on the Arkansas River takes its name from French *galets*, meaning "pebbles," and the outcropping may have been Galets de Rocher. The town of Galley or Galla Rock was established in 1840, with both spellings in use. To further muddle the record, a historical marker declares that the rock was "named after an Indian Chief or some say after 'The Galley' of a ship."

Hopefield Lake (Crittenden): An eighteenth-century Spanish outpost, Fort Esperanza, came under American occupation, becoming first Hope Encampment and later Hopefield. This was an important town on the Military Road and the eastern terminus of the first railroad to Little Rock. While the settlement was washed away in 1912, its name remains in that of the lake, also called Dacus Lake.

Kentucky (Saline): Settled in the 1820s by a number of families from Kentucky, who first called the town the Lindsey Community, then Caldwellton, and finally settled on Kentucky.

Lapile *luh-PEEL* (Union): A settlement was established in the 1840s, but a post office did not open until 1877. Deane is unsure whether the town's name is a French word for "pile" or some French trapper's name. Over the centuries, the name has also been spelled Lapeal or La Peil.

Marie Saline River: From French *marais salin*, "salt marsh."

Mount Magazine and town (Logan): The highest point in Arkansas. According to Thomas Nuttall, it was so named by the French because it looked like a barn (French *magasin*), and so early English-speaking residents called it Barn Mountain, then Magazine Mountain and finally Mount Magazine. The town was established after the Civil War as a stop on the Rock Island Railroad.

Mount Sequoyah (Washington): Deane notes that originally, this was the name of a retreat owned by the Western Methodist Assembly of the Methodist Episcopal Church, South and named in honor of the Cherokee leader. Eventually, it came to refer to the whole mountain.

Omaha (Boone): The town was established after the Civil War, and the only hint as to why the 1873 post office was so named is a local story that says there had been an American Indian village there named Sha-wa-nah.

Mount Magazine. *Courtesy of GoodFreePhotos.com.*

Osceola: One of the two seats of Mississippi County was founded in 1837 as Plum Point and, in 1853, renamed, like many other towns, for the Seminole chief. The legend that Osceola himself visited in 1832 has no evidence supporting it.

Ozan *oh-ZAN* (Hempstead): French explorers called this area Prairie d'Han ("Prairie of Caravansary") or Prairie aux Anes ("Prairie Near the Donkey"); therefore, Ozan may be a version of Aux Han or Aux Anes. Deane mentions, but does not cite, a researcher saying that French hunters of the Middle Ages would shout out "Han!" on felling a big animal. Another historian agrees that *han* is a French exclamation, but one made after an exertion—and in Caribbean French, an exclamation of surprise. How exactly any of these connect to a prairie is never explicated, and so the mystery remains.

Ozark *OH-zark*: One of the two seats of Franklin County, the town was settled early in the nineteenth century at a crossing point on the Arkansas River and was allegedly the first town to officially use the word *Ozark*. Scholars have developed no fewer than six different tales about the origin of this word, with no judgment on which is right. All involve the Americanization of the French phrase "Aux Arcs," short for "Aux Arkansas," the name given by early French settlers to the region. G.W. Featherstone, in his 1844 *Excursions through the Slave States*, gives as common knowledge that Aux Arcs was an abbreviation of Aux Arkansas, and there is evidence of an 1806 traveler calling Arkansas Post "Ozark."

Pair o'Geese Lake (Bradley): Also listed on United States Geological Survey maps as Peeregeethe. Deane traces this back to the French word for the Indian dugout canoe, *pirogue*, which has certainly been revised over the years.

Palarm *puh-LARM* (Faulkner): Deane attributes this name to the home of early settler Baptiste Larme, his Place des Larmes, which evolved to the modern spelling. Alas, there is no evidence that Larme was ever in Arkansas. Allsopp, for his part, blithely asks, "What was the cause of the alarm?"

Pee Dee (Van Buren): Deane logically attributes this to an 1860s settler from South Carolina.

Point Remove Creek (Conway): Despite popular belief, the creek—and the point where it empties into the Arkansas River—has nothing to do with the removal of American Indians or the Trail of Tears. The name probably derives from the French *remous*, meaning "eddy" or "whirlpool." An 1813 document refers to "point remove byo" (i.e., bayou), and an 1819 account by Thomas Nuttall refers to Point Remu. Finally, an 1820s narrative calls the site "Point Remove, or Eddy Point creek." All of these names were used well before the Indian removals.

Poison Spring State Park (Ouachita) and State Forest (Nevada): The name was in use in reports of the 1864 Civil War battle. There is a dubious tale about Union soldiers drinking from the springs and becoming ill, but more probably, the name has something to do with the French word for "fish," *poisson*.

Poteau River *POH-toh* (Scott and Sebastian): Traditionally, this name is attributed to the French word for trading post, *poteau*. Unfortunately for this theory, Dickinson points out that the French word for trading post is *poste*, and a *poteau* might have been a ceremonial wooden post.

Sabougla (Calhoun): Local lore says that this is a Choctaw or Cherokee word for "muddy water." Established in 1846 as Sabougly, the town's name got its current spelling when the post office was established in 1873.

Salado Creek and Village *SAL-uh-doh* (Independence): Early versions of the creek name started with Salido, then moved to Sallydoe and Sally-Doe. The village was established in the early nineteenth century, and the story is that a young woman named Sally, washing clothes in the creek, saw a deer and either shot it or beat it to death with her washboard, ergo "Sally killed a doe" or "Sally-doe." In fact, early maps show the creek named Sal d'Eau, or salty water. The bayou was first called Bayou Saladore, and Deane attributes this to the Spanish for "salty," *salado*, as there are numerous rivers and towns with this name in Spanish-speaking countries.

Shinall Mountain (Pulaski): Probably named—and then Americanized— for the French Chenault family that settled there.

Solgohachia *sahl-guh-HACH-ee* (Conway): Allegedly an Indian name meaning "hole in the mountain," because of a belief that there was a treasure buried there.

Tyronza, river and a Poinsett County town: The river, now much changed from its original form, may be the River of Casqui mentioned in the chronicles of Hernando de Soto. Local history, noting that the town's first house was built on the prominent Indian mound, says that Tyronza was an Indian chief.

Chapter 2

POLITICIANS, SOLDIERS AND SIGNIFICANT CITIZENS

E arly American places were very often named for important politicians who had directed their settlement: Kings (George and Charles) and queens (Mary) gave their names to colonies that eventually became states. American heroes like Washington and Franklin were celebrated in place names as the new nation pushed westward. As the states were divided into counties and towns sprang up, citizens of less stature but of national significance were celebrated.

In the young state of Arkansas, names of nationally prominent politicians and soldiers went to counties and county seats. Early counties named for presidents include Washington, Jefferson, Madison, Monroe, Van Buren, Jackson and Polk, while Greene, Pulaski, Lafayette, Marion and Montgomery Counties were named for Revolutionary War heroes.

New towns snatched at any names not already taken, and cabinet members or federal senators like John Randolph had counties and towns named for them. As more Arkansas counties were created, they often took the names of men with local significance, such as early governors and military heroes from the War of 1812 and the Mexican War and then from the Civil War. Both Confederate and Union leaders have their names on the map of Arkansas, based generally on when the place was organized: Reconstruction led to places being named for federal leaders, and the repeal of Reconstruction to southern generals being immortalized.

Abbott (Scott): First settled in the nineteenth century and originally called Black Jack, like the nearby ridge, which was probably named for the presence of black jack oaks. The town was established in 1899 and named for the Abbott family.

Adona (Perry): Originally called Cypress Valley; when a post office was established in 1879, the name became Adona to honor a relative of John Howell, the town's first permanent resident.

Alix (Franklin): An infamous sundown town, named for Constance (or Constant) Alix, who sold some property to the Little Rock & Fort Smith Railroad.

Almyra (Arkansas): In the middle of the Grand Prairie and built around 1890 on the Stuttgart and Arkansas Railroad, the settlement was named for Mrs. Almyra D. Dayer, sister of one of the town's property owners.

Anderson Flat (Marion): Established in the late nineteenth century on the unusually flat prairie and named for the resident who donated land for the public school. The post office, in the Verona General Store, was named **Verona**.

Ashley County: Chester Ashley was an early U.S. senator from Arkansas.

Atkins Lake (Jefferson): Sometimes spelled Adkins, formed when the Arkansas River shifted. Probably named for early Jefferson County settler George W. Atkins Sr., and so it was called by 1870.

Augusta: Seat of Woodruff County, it was originally named Chickasaw Landing, which was later changed to honor either Augusta Cald, niece of town founder Thomas Hough, or Augusta Huff, niece of Thomas Huff. There seems to have been a surfeit of Augustas thereabouts.

Barkada (Drew): Settled in the mid-nineteenth century and first called Cavaness Landing, which, in 1884, was changed to honor early settler James Barker. The *-ada* seems to have been added simply to modify the name and not—as some have theorized—to incorporate the name of a wife or daughter Ada (who didn't exist).

Barling (Sebastian): Aaron Barling purchased land eight miles east of Fort Smith in 1817 and founded the town of Spring Hill just outside what is now Fort Chaffee. Steady growth led to a post office in 1890, but since there was already a Spring Hill in White County, the town was renamed for its founder.

Barton (Phillips): Perhaps named for landowner Bart Green, one of a group of Swiss settlers on Crowley's Ridge.

Batesville: Seat of Independence County, at the fall line of the White River, and named in honor of James Woodson Bates, the first territorial delegate of Arkansas to the U.S. Congress. It has also been called Napoleon and Poke Bayou.

Baxter (Drew): Originally named Bartholomew, since it was on the bayou and was the northernmost port for steamboats. The name was changed during the Brooks-Baxter War to honor Elisha Baxter.

Baxter County: Arkansas governor Elisha Baxter formed this county in 1873 from four other counties through some legislative sleight of hand.

Beaver (Carroll): The town grew up around a trading post and ferry run by Wilson Asbury Beaver Sr.

Beedeville *BEE-di-vil* (Jackson): Named for William H. Beede, an early settler in the years after the Civil War.

Benton County: Named for Thomas H. Benton, a U.S. senator from Missouri who helped Arkansas attain statehood. The county seat, **Bentonville**, is also named for him, as is **Benton**, the seat of Saline County, which was settled in the 1830s. Some historians, oddly, credit federal general Thomas H. Benton. While not related to the senator, artist Thomas Hart Benton loved exploring the Arkansas Ozarks and was a powerful advocate for the preservation of the Buffalo River.

Berryville: One of the two seats of Carroll County, it was named for either founder Blackburn Henderson Berry or for his brother, Governor James H. Berry.

Bertig (Greene): Settled in the 1890s by Jewish businessman Adolph Bertig, who purchased a tram line from Paragould to his lumber mill on the St. Francis River. The town dwindled after 1915 and was destroyed by the 1927 flood.

Beverage Town (Van Buren): Not what it seems! The town was settled after 1850 and first called Gravel Hill for the local rocky hill on which it was built. Around 1921, Mr. Dempsey Beverage built a store there and, since his store probably held the post office, got the town renamed.

Bidville (Crawford): First called Shepherd Mountain and later named for prominent settler "Bid" Renfro.

Biggers (Randolph): The town was named for B.F. Bigger, who purchased land, built a ferry and constructed a distillery.

Blackton (Monroe): Settled in the second half of the nineteenth century. The original post office application in 1880 gave the name as Hickory Hills, which was changed in quick succession to Dunn and then to Blackton. One local story says that William Black of Brinkley built a railroad to the settlement to transport lumber for his mill.

Blansett *BLAN-suht* (Scott): First settled around 1840 by the Gist family but named for Jim Blansett, an early settler and reputed bushwhacker.

Blevins *BLE-vunz* (Hempstead): Named for early settlers Hugh and Sarah Blevins and Hugh's brother Dillen.

Blytheville *BLEYEDH-vil:* One of two seats of Mississippi County, the town was founded around 1880 by Methodist circuit rider Henry T. Blythe, who was also the town's first postmaster and owner of a steam-powered sawmill and gin. He allegedly wanted to name the settlement Blythe but was dissuaded, and it was originally called Blythesville.

Boles (Scott): Settled around 1840 and first called Stringtown, possibly because travel along the nearby Fourche La Fave River involved using rope strung along the river bank. The Boles family settled there in the 1860s, eventually giving their name to the town.

Bolivar: Established in 1838 as the Poinsett County seat and named for Joel Poinsett's hero, Simon Bolivar. The town rapidly declined when the seat was moved to Harrisonburg, and it was destroyed by the Civil War.

Bono (Faulkner): Settled in the late nineteenth century and called Kendall, for the first postmaster. The town later changed its name to honor early settler William Bono, who had Anglicized his name from the French Bonneau.

Boone County: Established in 1869; most—including the contemporary *Arkansas Gazette*—say it was named for Daniel Boone. Others of an imaginative bent say that residents hoped the new county would be a boon for them, and there's no denying that there was significant variation in the county itself over the spelling.

Booneville *BOON-vuhl:* One of Logan County's two seats, with two stories about its name. One says that early settler Walter Cauthron called it Bonneville, for his friend Captain Benjamin Bonneville. The other story is that Daniel Boone was a kinsman of the Logan family, for whom the county is named, and the town was named in his honor.

Boxley (Newton): The town was established in the 1840s and first called Whiteley's Mill for the owner of a small mill. The name was changed in 1883 to honor a more successful miller named William Boxley.

Branch (Franklin): Established in 1898 as the terminus for the Arkansas Central Railroad in coal country and supposed to have been called Turner for one of the founders. But because of the Turner in Phillips County, the settlers themselves opted for another founder, John Branch.

Brownstown (Sevier): First settled around 1830 as Pine Woods, the town later changed its name in honor of early settler Henry K. Brown.

Brownsville (Lonoke): Founded in the 1840s and named for Major Jacob Brown of Little Rock, an early casualty in the Mexican War. The town was devastated by the Civil War and eventually abandoned after the Memphis & Little Rock Plank Road or Railroad missed the town by three miles.

Cammack Village (Pulaski): A suburb of Little Rock, created in 1943 as a site for federally subsidized housing on land owned by Wiley Dan Cammack.

The village has never been annexed into Little Rock, which completely surrounds it.

Capps (Boone): Robert Capps was an early settler in the county. Originally called Mountain Spring, the town was renamed after the railroad came through in 1905.

Caraway (Craighead): What began as a lumber camp around 1912 and was known as White Switch quickly grew. The town got its post office in 1916 and was renamed in honor of long-serving U.S. senator Thaddeus Caraway and his wife, Hattie, who succeeded him in the Senate.

Carpenter Dam: Flavius Josephus Carpenter, an officer with Arkansas Power & Light, selected the location for the dam on the Ouachita River. Deane, however, prefers a story that identifies Carpenter as a riverboat captain who came up with the idea for the dam.

Carroll County and **Carrollton**: Both the county and the town were named for Charles Carroll of Carrollton, Maryland, a signer of the Declaration of Independence.

Casscoe or **Cascoe** *KASS-koh* (Monroe): An early, and perhaps the first, settlement on the White River. Its 1851 name, according to local history, combined the names of two of Jackson's staff officers at the Battle of New Orleans, General Cass and Colonel Coe. Neither name can be verified, but it's still a nice etymology. Twenty years later, the name was changed to Wellborn by prominent citizen Isaac Starnes Welborn III. Around 1882, the name was changed to Bermuda, ostensibly (and surely impossibly) because of the lush Bermuda grass, but eventually, sensible heads restored the name Casscoe.

Cauthron (Scott): Established after the Civil War, the town was first called Piney and later renamed for Judge Joe Cauthron from Sebastian County.

Charleston: One of the two seats of Franklin County, the town was settled around 1870 and named Charles Town for one of its early settlers, Charles R. Kellum, a Baptist preacher, store owner and the first postmaster. In 1874, after Kellum had moved away, the name was changed to its current form.

Charlotte *SHAR-luht* (Independence): Established in the mid-nineteenth century by James N. Churchill and named for his wife, Charlotte.

Chidester (Ouachita): In 1880, the St. Louis, Iron Mountain and Southern Railroad bought land for a depot along a spur and laid out plans for a town, which was eventually named for prominent Camden citizen John T. Chidester.

Clarendon: The seat of Monroe County, established where the road from Memphis to Little Rock crossed the White River. Early on, it was called Mouth of the Cache, then Rockroe or Roe Rock. Deane says that it was named for the Earl of Clarendon but doesn't explain why.

Clark County: Named for William Clark, the famous explorer and governor of the Missouri Territory.

Clarksville: The seat of Johnson County was established in 1836, and an early story says it was named for a nearby settler, General Lorenzo Clark. But a better and more likely story is that the town was built on land named for one of the three current county commissioners in the hope—apparently realized!—of gaining his support for locating the county seat there.

Claybrook (Crittenden): The town's name, originally Topaz, was changed to honor local Black entrepreneur John C. Claybrook.

Cleburne County *KLEE-burn:* The last-formed of Arkansas' counties, it was created in 1883 and named for Irish immigrant and Confederate general Patrick Cleburne. An early tale that it was named for an ancestor of Cleburne is clearly, as Cleburne himself might say, malarkey.

Cleveland County: Formed in 1873 as Dorsey County, it was named for Republican congressman Stephen Dorsey. Dorsey's short stint in the U.S. Senate is remembered for his having Washington's birthday declared a holiday and for his corruption. In 1885, after Dorsey's reputation was in tatters, the name was changed to honor newly sworn-in U.S. president Grover Cleveland.

Cleveland (Conway): Settled in the 1880s and named for President Grover Cleveland, who had signed the homestead certificates.

Colburn Spring (Scott): A settlement grew up after the Civil War around a spring named for the Coburns, a family of early settlers, but no one knows when or how the *l* got added.

Collins (Drew): The town was founded around 1850 and first called Cut-Off, being on Cut-Off Creek, but the name was later changed to honor early settler General Benjamin F. Collins.

Collum (Van Buren County): First called Chalk, probably for the families of Green Chalk and W.B. Chalk, but when they moved on, the town changed its name to honor settlers George and Mary Collum, who had come from Oklahoma around 1874.

Conway County: Established in 1825 and named for Henry Wharton Conway, a young territorial delegate to the U.S. House of Representatives.

Conway (Faulkner): Established after the Civil War, the town was, unlike Conway County, named for the family of James Sevier Conway, the state's first elected governor. One story maintains that Asa Robinson, owner of the Little Rock & Fort Smith Railroad Company, had long planned a station there and named it for the first of his locomotives to arrive in 1870. Any connection between the locomotive's name and the family is tenuous at best.

Cord (Independence): Developed in the early nineteenth century and originally called Hopewell. The 1880 post office was named Cord, perhaps to honor the locally prominent farming family of John W. McCord.

Corley (Logan): The town grew up around Burnette Springs, named for an early settler, and became a summer resort. Eventually, the town was named for an even earlier settler, John Corley, who was a Unionist and was hanged by bushwhackers in 1864.

Crabtree (Van Buren): This town was named not for a tree but for early settler Jim Crabtree from South Carolina.

Craighead County: Established in 1858 and perversely named for Thomas Craighead, a state senator who opposed creation of the county. (*See* Jonesboro.)

Crawford County: Named for William H. Crawford of Georgia, then U.S. secretary of the treasury.

Crittenden County *KRIT-uhn-duhn:* Named for Robert Crittenden, first secretary of the Arkansas Territory.

Crockett's Bluff (Arkansas): First called Hillsboro; local legend says it was renamed for Davy Crockett. But in fact, there were several Crocketts living there, including a David Crockett who owned a large farm.

Cross County: Formed in 1862 and named for local planter Colonel David C. Cross, CSA, or possibly for Edward Cross, an Arkansas Supreme Court justice and early advocate for railroads.

Crowley's Ridge *KROH-liz:* A long ridge named for Benjamin Crowley, an early and prominent settler, as is the state park where his home and grave are located.

Cypert (Phillips): Established in the mid-nineteenth century, it was originally called Coffee Creek, allegedly because a teamster, trying to cross the swollen creek, lost a wagonload of coffee beans, which remained in the creek for a few years. The 1866 application for a post office called the settlement Cypert after circuit judge J.N. Cypert of Searcy, instead of the spilled beans.

Dallas (Polk): The county's first seat was established in the mid-nineteenth century and named, as was **Dallas County**, for James K. Polk's vice president, George Dallas of Pennsylvania.

Datto *DAT-oh* (Clay): Around 1900, the town of Thurman, in order to be closer to the railroad, moved a mile north to the land of Isaac Day. Deane says that his name was J.H. Day, a sawmill operator who named the community Day Town or Dayton. The Post Office said no, so Datto came about as a compromise.

Davidsonville (Randolph): An important town in early Arkansas history, it existed in the first half of the nineteenth century and was named for legislator John Davidson.

Datto. *Courtesy of Brian Stansberry. Own work, CC BY 4.0, https://commons. wikimedia.org/w/index. php?curid=90998875.*

Deans Market (Crawford): This town may be connected to a Dean Springs named for early settler Elisher Preston Dean.

Decatur (Benton): Established after the Civil War and first called Corner Springs. In 1882, when the USPS rejected that name, settler Everard Mitchell suggested the name Mitchell, which was also rejected. He then proposed naming it after a hero of the War of 1812, Stephen Decatur, who had family in the area.

Dennard (Van Buren): Hugh Dennard, an Englishman who came for a visit to the home of Josh Buchannon, stayed to become the first schoolteacher. Although Dennard suggested the name Buchannon, the townsfolk so admired him that they chose his name.

Dermott *DURR-maht* (Chicot): Dr. Charles McDermott established a plantation there in 1844 and was a beloved physician.

Desha County: *DEE-SHAY* or *duh-SHAY*: Named for Captain Benjamin Desha, a soldier in the War of 1812.

Desha (Independence): Founded in the early nineteenth century and first called Alderbrook. In 1883, it was named in honor of Franklin W. Desha, veteran of the Mexican and Civil Wars and a local leader.

De Valls Bluff: One of the seats of Prairie County, settled just before the Civil War and named for Jacob M. DeVall, the first European settler.

Dewey (White): The town's post office opened in 1898 and was named for Admiral George Dewey, victor at the recent Battle of Manila Bay in the Spanish-American War.

DeWitt *de-WITT* or *DEE-witt:* One of the two Arkansas County seats and named for New York politician DeWitt Clinton. The story is that the three commissioners who selected the site each wrote a prospective town name on a slip of paper, and that of surveyor McCool, who had written "Clinton," was drawn. But since there was already a Clinton, the town was called DeWitt.

Dowdy (Independence): Developed in the second half of the nineteenth century, the town had quite a series of names: Pansy, McGill, Lockhart/Lockheart Point, Black River and its current form, for Batesville merchant R.A. Dowdy.

Dumas *DOO-muss* (Desha): Settled in the late nineteenth century and named for local landowner William B. Dumas, who perhaps was a county surveyor and laid out the town.

Entering Dumas from the north. *Courtesy of Brandonrush. Own work, CC BY-SA 3.0, https://commons.wikimedia.org/w/index.php?curid=19492505.*

Dyer (Crawford): Joel Dyer built a farm next to the Military Road in the 1840s and offered a rest stop for wagon trains. When the Little Rock & Fort Smith Railroad built a depot there in 1876, it was called Dyer Station, and the town grew after that.

Dyess *DYE-es* (Mississippi): A "resettlement colony" established during the Great Depression, incorporated in 1936. It was named for W.R. Dyess, the WPA administrator for Arkansas, a local plantation owner and originator of the idea of the resettlement colonies.

Earle (Crittenden): Logging community formed in the late nineteenth century. When the railroad came through, the widow of Confederate cavalry officer Josiah Earle allowed a depot to be built on her property.

Elaine *EE-lane* (Phillips): A railroad depot was established in 1906 and originally named Kelley by the property owner, Harry Kelley. But because there was another depot named Kelley, he changed the name—either to one of his daughters' or, as some wags said, a popular actress's.

Elizabeth (Jackson): This early seat of Jackson County, a busy port on the White River, was named for two settlers' wives, one named Elizabeth and the other a native of Elizabeth, New Jersey. Flooding led to the town's demise in the 1850s.

Ellsworth (Logan): Settled before the Civil War, Ellsworth became the seat of Sarber County in 1873 and finally withered away in the 1930s. It was probably named for U.S. Supreme Court chief justice Oliver Ellsworth.

Emerson (Calhoun): Although many residents called it Reuben, the depot on the Louisiana and Arkansas Railroad finally took on the family name of local politician Reuben Logan Emerson around 1900.

Enders *IN-duhrs* (Faulkner): Although the first settlement dated to the 1840s, the town only sought a post office in 1880, as Sulphur Springs. Because there already was a Sulphur Springs in Arkansas, the USPS rejected that name. The residents then named the town for townsman Jordan Enders Craven.

England (Lonoke): Settled around 1880 and originally called Groveland, although there is also evidence for the name Hurgens. In 1888, after the railroad came through, the town was platted and named for John Calhoun England, a landowner and lawyer for the Cotton Belt Railroad who had purchased much of the land along the rail line. The USPS initially refused to change the name because of its official policy not to name towns after foreign countries but eventually relented.

Eros (Marion): One local historian guesses that the name is the Greek *eros*, but it may also be just a revision of the name of the Rose family.

Eudora (Chicot): A church and a Masonic lodge were established in the 1840s, and a growing settlement was named after nearby Eudora Plantation. That farm was named by owner E.C. James for his daughter Frances Eudora, who died in 1858 at age four. The town's name was briefly changed to Carmel from around 1890 until the railroad came through in 1903, when the name was changed back. Deane relates another story that says the town was simply named for the daughter of Dr. S.A. Scott, an early settler.

Faulkner County: Named for Sanford C. "Sandy" Faulkner, who, among other things, composed the song "The Arkansas Traveler."

Fayetteville: The seat of Washington County and originally called Washington Courthouse. This was changed in 1829 to avoid confusion with the Washington in Hempstead County. The new name was suggested by two county commissioners who had come from Fayetteville, Tennessee, which itself had been named for Fayetteville, North Carolina, which had been named for the Marquis de Lafayette.

Fendley (Clark): Settled in the 1870s by the Fendley family, and the 1901 post office was headed by Thomas M. Fendley.

Ferda (Jefferson): Perhaps named for Ferda Harvis, son of Ferdinand (Ferd) Harvis, longtime Jefferson County Republican leader.

Finch (Greene): Settled in the 1870s and named for the town's first schoolmaster.

Flippin. *Courtesy of U.S. Environmental Protection Agency.*

Flippin (Marion): When it was settled in the early 1800s, the town was first called the Barrens. Then, for a while, the settlement was called Goatville for a goat that allegedly butted out of town a dishonest peddler. Thomas H. Flippin became an important citizen in the 1840s, and the town's name was changed first to Flippin Barrens, then officially to Flippin in 1921.

Floral (Independence): Established after the Civil War and named either for local flowers or a Floral family that lived there.

Foreman (Little River): A settlement grew up in the early nineteenth century around a spring and was named Willow Springs. By 1850, it was called Rocky Comfort, allegedly because that is what the local American Indians had called it. This was not because rocks have traditionally been sources of comfort but on account of the spring issuing from limestone, which created a watering hole for buffalo and other animals. The Arkansas & Choctaw Railroad built a depot about a mile north of the town, and merchants moved there, calling the place New Rocky Comfort. The railroad depot and post office were officially named Foreman for Ben Foreman, a civic leader in Texarkana, but residents (and the federal census) used both names until about 1960.

Forester (Scott): Established in 1930 as a logging town and named for Waldron businessman Charles A. Forrester. Somewhere along the way, an *r* went missing.

Forrest City: The seat of St. Francis County was established after the Civil War as a commissary for workers on the Memphis and Little Rock Railroad, who were under the supervision of Confederate cavalry commander and landowner Nathan Bedford Forrest. V.B. Izard laid out the town, which was almost called Izardtown, but since the depot had been informally called Forrest's Town for years, that name stuck.

Fort Chaffee (Sebastian): Built in 1941 and named for Major General Adna R. Chaffee, an artillery officer in World War I who was an early advocate for tanks.

Fort Smith: One of two county seats for Sebastian County, the military post was set up in 1817 at Belle Point and named for General Thomas Adams Smith, the military district commander, who never visited the fort.

Fouke (Miller): In 1887, a Seventh Day Baptist congregation was looking for a place where they could practice their faith, and Presbyterian lumberman George W. Fouke invited them to settle near his sawmill, the terminal of the grandly named Texarkana, Shreveport and Natchez Railroad. The town is famous as the center of the territory of the Fouke Monster, which generated excitement when it was allegedly seen nearby in 1971 and became the subject of a low-budget pseudo-documentary film .

Fox (Stone): Homesteaded after the Civil War and originally called Smart. Another name was needed for the post office in 1905: one story says that someone caught a fox in the middle of town, but a more likely tale says that the town was named after a Fox family.

French Prairie (Logan): One delightful story is that the Quapaws were so impressed with the skills of the French trappers that the Indians themselves named the area for them. In fact, it was almost certainly named for some of the earliest White settlers, the Walter French and Samuel French families.

Fulton County: Formed in 1842 from Izard County and named for William S. Fulton, the last governor of the Arkansas Territory and a U.S. senator.

Fulton (Hempstead): Established shortly after 1800 where the Southwest Trail crossed the Red River and, by 1806, known as Fulton. Some say it honors William S. Fulton, others say Robert Fulton of steamboat fame and no one knows for sure.

Garfield (Benton): Established in 1881 as a depot at the highest point on the St. Louis–San Francisco Railroad in Benton County and first called Blansett for a local store owner. The name was then quickly changed to Crowell by the postmaster, Samuel Crowell. In 1883, the town was platted, and the railroad asked that the name be changed to honor slain president James Garfield, although the official name change did not occur until 1887.

Garland County: Named for Augustus Hill Garland, a Confederate congressman, governor of Arkansas, U.S. senator and then attorney general under Grover Cleveland.

Garland (Miller): The town on the Red River that finally got its post office in 1883 under the name of Garland had long been called Lost Prairie, since much of its land was so often flooded by the Great Raft. One early store owner was Rufus Garland, father of Augustus, and it was in his honor that the town was finally officially named.

Georgetown (White): Settled in 1789 by Francis Francure and originally called Francure Township. From 1870 to 1909, the post office was officially Negro Hill and sometimes, locally, Nigger Hill, possibly because of a nearby settlement of formerly enslaved persons from Louisiana. The current name came in 1909 from three men surnamed George who invested in developing the town around 1900.

Gid (Izard): After the Civil War, blacksmith Gideon "Gid" (or "Uncle Gid") Bruce set up shop here and became a pillar of the town. One cold morning in 1888, Bruce came into the store of postmaster John Hanna to warm up as a group of men sitting around the stove were arguing about what to name the post office, and they quickly agreed on the nickname of the blacksmith.

Gosnell (Mississippi): Settled early in the twentieth century, originally called Chickasawba for reasons not known and later named for early settler Lemael Gosnell, a dentist and farmer.

Grady (Lincoln): Settled in the mid-nineteenth century, the town was originally called Hall's Landing, then Williamsburg. In 1898, the town changed its name to Grady to honor the local telegraph operator.

Grant County: Formed in 1869 from parts of Jefferson, Hot Spring and Saline Counties and named for Union general Ulysses Grant. Early attempts by disgruntled residents to change the name did not succeed.

Gravette *GRA-vutt* (Benton): E.T. Gravett ran a distillery in the biblically named town of Nebo. But when the railroad bypassed Nebo, Gravett moved his distillery to the tracks, and the rest of the town soon followed. Gravett had dropped the final *e* from his family name, owing to some family argument, but included it in the town's name, which became official with the 1893 post office.

Greenwood: One of two seats of Sebastian County, it was established in 1851 on the banks of the Vache Grasse Creek and named for Judge Alfred Burton Greenwood.

Greers Ferry Dam, Lake and town (Cleburne): A dam built in the early 1960s was named for a nineteenth-century ferry that was operated in the area by William V. (Bud) Greer until 1890. The town was formed by area residents displaced by the rising water of the lake.

Grubbs (Jackson): Established around 1880 as an agricultural town and named for local citizen James C. Grubbs.

Hackett (Sebastian): Jeremiah Hackett established the town in 1834 and named it Hickory Grove. In 1876, when the town decided to incorporate, the residents voted for Hackett City over Johnson, and the "City" was dropped by the USPS.

Halley *HAL-lee* (Desha): When the station on the Mississippi, Ouachita & Red River Railroad was built, it was called Bowie's Station for a nearby farmer. Eventually, the line moved a mile north, and a new station was called Halley's Station for a prominent (and numerous) family headed by Hillard Halley.

Hamlett (Faulkner): The story is that it was settled around 1905 and named for an early family, the Hamletts.

Hampton: The Calhoun County seat was founded shortly after 1850 and was named for state senator Colonel John R. Hampton.

Harkey Valley (Yell): Also called Harkey's Valley, it was named for the Harkey family, who settled in the area in the middle of the nineteenth century.

Harrell (Calhoun): Built about 1900, the railroad depot was first called Rolyart, then Harrell in honor of Martha Wood Harrell, who operated a boardinghouse near the railroad.

Harriet (Searcy): In 1908, the Andersons from Missouri, according to the family story, settled here and requested a post office. The local postal representative came and was served homemade bread and a delicious strawberry pie by Harriet Esther Anderson, who was deaf. The postal representative knew sign language, so they had a nice conversation, and upon his return to his office, he had the post office named for her.

Harrisburg (Poinsett): The Harris family, which would include state senator Benjamin Harris and the first county judge, William Harris, settled here in the 1830s. Twenty years later, it became the county seat.

Harrison: The seat of Boone County was settled in the 1830s and originally called Beller Stand, possibly for the Beller family's deer stand. In 1836, the town became Crooked Creek, and in 1870, it was renamed in honor of Marcus LaRue Harrison, colonel of the First Arkansas Cavalry (U.S.), who had surveyed and platted the new part of the town.

Hartford (Sebastian): Settled before the Civil War by C.E. Goddard, who had come back from the California Gold Rush, and briefly called Old Sugarloaf Valley. The settlement was soon called Hart's Ford for the family, or perhaps for the widow Hart, who lived near the crossing of West Creek. A few miles away, a mining settlement first called Center Point was established and later named Gwyn for local landowner and/or coal mine owner Wylie P. Gwyn, or Gwynn. After the Choctaw-Memphis Railroad came through, the town that grew up next to the railroad was called either

Gwyn or New Hartford, and the older town became Old Hartford or West Hartford. By 1905, the new town was simply Hartford.

Haskell (Saline): The town formed around a depot built to serve two railroads in the 1880s. Haskell Dickinson, who had donated land for the depot, became the first postmaster and gave his name to the town.

Heber Springs *HEE-ber:* The seat of Cleburne County. The local springs attracted land speculation, and a town encompassing them was originally called Magness Springs, then later Sugar Loaf by the city founder, Max Frauenthal, because of its proximity to Sugar Loaf Mountain. In 1910, to avoid confusion with another Sugar Loaf, Frauenthal changed the name to honor Dr. Heber Jones, a Memphis physician and son of a town founder.

Helena: The county seat of Phillips County was platted in 1820, incorporated in 1833 and named after the daughter of Sylvanus Phillips, who had given his name to the county. Deane says that the settlement was originally called Monticello, then St. Francis, since the St. Francis River joined the Mississippi nearby.

Hempstead County: Named for Edward Hempstead, the first delegate to the U.S. House of Representatives from the Missouri Territory.

Hickman (Clark): One of several places named for Dr. Elliott Hickman, the others being Hickman Bend and Hickman Landing on the Mississippi.

Highfill (Benton): The town of Hoover, named for the young Stanford University student named Herbert Hoover who had surveyed the area in the 1890s, was bypassed by the Rogers Southwestern Railroad. The residents moved a mile or two to land owned by Hezekiah Highfill next to the tracks, and the town was platted in 1906.

Holland (Faulkner): Established early in the nineteenth century by English settlers and seemingly named not for the country but for a hunter and trapper who had camped thereabouts.

Holub (Lee): Established around 1910 and named for settler Joe Holub.

Hon *HAHN* (Scott): Established in 1836 by Jackson Hon, and first called Valley Forge and then Poteau, Hon was eventually named for Jackson's son, John.

Horatio (Sevier): Early in the nineteenth century, a small town named Rock Hill was settled, and prosperity finally arrived with the Texarkana & Fort Smith Railroad around 1900. The railroad's general manager, Fred Hubbell, named the town for his father, Horatio Hubbell. But perhaps a dispute concerning a bridge over the Little River reminded residents of the Roman hero Horatio, who had stood fast on the bridge.

Howard County: Formed in 1873 from Pike, Hempstead, Polk and Sevier Counties and named for James H. Howard, the state senator from the district when the county was formed.

Hughes (St. Francis): Established after 1910 on the Marianna Cut-Off of the Missouri-Pacific Railroad and named not for the local family of farmers but for Mississippian Robert Hughes, who had purchased the land where the town was developed.

Hunter (Woodruff): Settled after the Civil War by Edward Shannon Hunt, an Ohio soldier who returned to Arkansas after the war. His wife set up a wayside inn, which became known as Hunt's Station and gradually—and interestingly—Hunter.

Huntington (Sebastian): The town was established in the 1890s to support workers at three local coal mines and named for a mine superintendent who was killed when his horse jumped off a bridge.

Huttig (Union): C.D. Johnson established a town to support his lumber company and named it for his friend, industrialist William Huttig. Deane says that he named it for Charles Huttig, a banker from St. Louis.

Jamestown (Independence): This small town was established in the mid-nineteenth century and originally called Alderbrook. The name was changed around 1880, ostensibly in reference to historic Jamestown, Virginia, but more probably to honor Daniel James, who donated land for a church and Masonic hall.

Japton (Madison): A crossroads settled around 1890 had at its center a store owned by Jasper Monroe "Jap" Neal, and so the place became known as Jap's Town.

Jenny Lind (Sebastian): Settled in the 1850s. Deane reasonably guesses that the Swedish soprano was the inspiration. Allsopp muses that the singer probably never even knew of the town's existence and savors the fact that the town once had a prominent store named Lickskillett.

Johnson County: Named for Benjamin Johnson, a territorial judge.

Johnson (Washington): After the Civil War, J.Q. and B.F. Johnson took over ownership of the local mill, around which a settlement developed. Local farmers turned their strawberry crops into enough profit that the Frisco Railroad built a line to Johnson Switch, which in 1886 became simply Johnson.

Johnsville (Bradley): The oft-told story says that the name of the town was agreed on because so many—one list has four—of the original settlers were named John.

Joiner (Mississippi): Established as a railroad depot in 1903, incorporated in 1922 and named for either the Rufus L. Joiner family or for Dr. D.C. Joyner. Or perhaps both!

Jonesboro: One of the two seats of Craighead County, it was named for state senator William A. Jones, who had spearheaded the creation of the county. Some say that fellow senator Thomas Craighead, who had not wanted the county named for him, proposed the name, either in retaliation or appreciation. Another story is that the name, originally spelled Jonesborough, was proposed by the grateful citizens of the town, but the first story is better.

Judsonia *jud-SOHN-yuh* (White): Settled in the 1840s on the Little Red River, the town was first known as Prospect Bluff, although it has been noted that there was no bluff and little prospect. After the Civil War, Baptist families from the North established a town and college named for missionary to Burma Adoniram Judson just to the north of Prospect Bluff. The towns were combined in 1874 and given the current name.

Keo (Lonoke): The town of Cobb Settlement or Cobbs was established about 1880, but when the railroad passed a mile south, much of the town moved and made a new settlement named for Keo Dooley, daughter of local judge P.C. Dooley.

Kessler Mountain (Washington): Named for Phillip Kessler, who purchased property on the top of the mountain in 1866 and set up a vineyard and winery.

Kingston (Madison): Laid out in 1853 as Kings River, the town has a couple of stories behind its name, as told by Deane. The traditional derivation is from Mr. King Johnson, who was said to have built the first house, but research by high school students could not locate him in any census records. And while Henry King from Alabama had explored the region in the 1820s, it seems more likely that the town was named for one of the families named King that was living in the area.

Lacey (Drew): When it was settled around 1850, the town was first called Lick Skillet, then Slab Town for the slabs cut by E.D. Lacey's sawmill. While Lacey is clearly the source of the name, a popular alternative tale says that store owner William B. Daniel once mistakenly ordered so much lace from New Orleans that his store was called Lacey.

Lamar (Johnson): Samuel Adams established a farm in 1835, which was eventually named Stream of Cabins owing to the numerous cabins he built for his enslaved workers. As a settlement took shape, it was called Cabin Creek, but when the town was incorporated in 1887, it chose the name Lamar to honor Lucius Quintus Cincinnatus Lamar of Mississippi. The railroad depot continued to be called Cabin Creek for many years.

Lawrence County: Named for James Lawrence, a naval officer during the War of 1812 who had been killed in a duel with a British ship and before dying cried, "Don't give up the ship."

Lee's Creek: There is a very old story of a fight between Cherokee and Osage Indians, in which a White man named Lee was mortally wounded and died by the creek. The Indians called the creek Tu-yah-ho-sah, "where something dies," but Lee's name was easier for the White settlers.

Leola (Grant): Settled originally in the 1840s and known consecutively as New Prospect, Tuckerfield and Sandy Springs. When it was incorporated in 1907, the town was named Leola in memory of a girl, Alice Leola Cunningham, who is said to have died in a fire.

Leslie (Searcy): Settled in the mid-nineteenth century and originally called Wiley's Cove, it was renamed Leslie in 1887. Some say this was for Colonel Sam Leslie, who had been a militia commander in the Civil War, while others say it was for his brother, "Old Jack" Leslie.

Levesque *luh-VESK* (Cross): First called Magnolia Grove, the town eventually took a name honoring Captain James Levesque, a prominent citizen after the Civil War.

Lewisville: The seat of Lafayette County was settled around 1836 by Lewis Barnes Fort and almost immediately called Lewisville. Much of the town moved a bit to the south after the railroad came through in 1895, leading to an Old Lewisville and a New Lewisville. Eventually, the latter dropped the "New," and the location of Old Lewisville is not marked anywhere.

Lexa (Phillips): When the St. Louis, Iron Mountain and Southern Railroad came through this area in 1880, using land owned by Nathaniel Lexington Graves, a post office was built and given the name Lexington. Local history notes that in 1885, the name was officially shortened "with some difficulty" to Lexa, and Deane says that Lex was the name of Graves's son.

Light (Greene): First called by the French term Cache, the settlement was later named for merchant Warner or Benjamin Light when the town prospered in the late nineteenth century.

Lincoln County: Formed in 1871 from parts of Arkansas, Bradley, Desha, Drew and Jefferson Counties and named for Abraham Lincoln.

Lincoln (Washington): Originally and interestingly called Blackjack when it was organized in the 1870s near some blackjack trees. In the 1880s, some began to call the settlement Georgetown. But the post office rejected this name in 1885, and the postmaster selected Lincoln, a choice that was, unsurprisingly, not universally appreciated by the residents. There are two stories of how he chose the name, a curious one involving "a box of freight" and a more probable one about honoring the slain president.

Logan County: When established in 1871, it was called Sarber County for the state senator who helped guide the legislation. After Reconstruction, it was renamed for James Logan, an early settler.

Logoly State Park (Columbia): Land including a health resort was leased to the Boy Scouts and then became a state park. The families from Magnolia that owned the land—and gave parts of their names to the park—were the Longinos, Goodes and Lyles.

Lonsdale (Garland): John Gerdes Lonsdale Sr., a Hot Springs banker, founded this community in the second half of the nineteenth century, and the name became official in 1900.

Lurton (Newton): According to local history, the town was established in 1917, named by its first postmistress Cornelia Sutton in honor of a certain Marion Lurton, and the rest of that story needs telling.

Luxora (Mississippi): A prosperous river town founded after the Civil War and called Elmot because it was near the Elmot Sand Bar in the Mississippi. When the town was incorporated, its name was changed to honor Luxora Waller, the four-year-old daughter of a prominent early settler. Little Luxora, in turn, was named after a character in a novel.

McCrory (Woodruff): Founded in 1887 as a railroad station and named for a local landowner and early settler, Wade McCrory. The station was built near the location of a short-lived town with the fascinating name Jennie's Colony.

McGehee *muh-GEE* (Desha): Benjamin McGehee established a farm in 1857, and his son Abner owned the part of the farm where the railroad went through in 1878. Abner became the first postmaster in 1879.

McNeil (Columbia): The town of Gobold was first settled in the 1850s but changed its name to College Hill after early settler William B. McNeill opened a school there. A St. Louis, Arkansas & Texas Railroad station in the 1880s was named McNeil (minus an *l*)—as, eventually, was the town.

Magness (Independence): Established in 1882 as a railroad depot and named for the family of Colonel Morgan Magness, an early settler in the area.

Marhattianna (Marion): Unique in all of the United States, the town was named for Colonel W.A. Webber's three daughters, Mary, Hattie and Anna.

Marianna (Lee): Founded in 1848 on land sold by Mary Ann Harland, who had opposed the sale until she was told that the town would, according to one story, be named for her. Another version says that the town was named for her daughters, Mary and Anna. In any case, the residents quickly determined that the land was too prone to flooding, so in 1852, they moved three miles to a drier place, where they set up a new town but kept the old name.

Marion County: Formed in 1835, initially named for South Carolina's Revolutionary War hero Francis Marion and almost immediately renamed Searcy County by the Territorial General Assembly. The next year, on receiving a petition from residents, the state's First General Assembly restored the original name.

Marmaduke (Greene): Established in 1882 as a depot along a narrow-gauge railroad of the Cotton Belt Railroad and named, in gratitude, for Confederate general and Missouri governor John S. Marmaduke, who had camped in this area during the war and attempted to rein in the havoc wrought by local guerrillas.

Marshall: The seat of Searcy County was established in 1856 and named Burrowsville for Crawford County leader Napoleon Bonaparte Burrows. In the tense years after the Civil War, local Unionists pushed to have the name changed to honor early U.S. Supreme Court chief justice John Marshall, which was approved in 1867. A more arcane tale says that it was named for another John Marshall, one of the commissioners who had previously designated Raccoon Springs as the county seat.

Martinville (Faulkner): Originally known as Cadron Cove, the settlement was renamed by members of the Christadelphian sect in 1887 for two local leaders, brothers James Daniel and W.W. Martin.

Marvell *MAR-vuhl* (Phillips): Founded in the 1870s as a railroad depot on land owned by Colonel Marvell M. Carruth.

Massey Mountain (Van Buren): A ridge near Scotland, named not for its bulk but for early settler Henry Massey.

Maynard *MAY-nuhrd* (Randolph): Merchant John Maynard set up his shop in the 1870s at an important crossroads. Maynard suggested for the growing settlement the name of New Prospect, but the USPS rejected this all-too-common name in 1885, and so his name was selected for the town.

Maysville (Benton): Settled around 1830 and named Beatie's Prairie for the first settler, Adam Beatie. In 1850, the name was changed to honor another early settler, John Martin May.

Menifee (Conway): A railroad station in the 1870s, named for property owner Dr. Nimrod Menifee, which turned into a town.

Miller County: The original boundaries of the county, when it was formed in 1820, extended far into what was then Mexico and is now Texas. Upon Texas gaining statehood in 1836, the county ceased to exist, but it was reestablished in 1874 and named for James Miller, the first and perhaps the most ineffective governor of the Arkansas Territory.

Milligan Ridge (Mississippi): The Milligans were a family on the run from the law when they settled here in the late nineteenth century. They established a homestead, and over time, a small town grew up to support lumber companies and sharecroppers.

Montgomery Point (Desha): Deane notes that in the nineteenth century, another Richard Montgomery ran "a fine public house" and so gave his name to the point, also called Montgomery Landing, as well as to Montgomery Towhead and Montgomery Island.

Moro *MOH-roh* (Lee): Two towns in Hampton Township have been named Moro. The first Moro was founded in 1835, and according to local lore, it was named by early settler Dr. James A. Sullivan for a Moro Bay in England. Alas, there is no such place in England, so perhaps it was named for **Moro Bay** in Bradley County. This inlet on the Ouachita River is identified in an

1804 document as "Bay Morau." Deane surmises that the name evolved from the French *moreau*, meaning "dark," and had to do with "the dark creek water." But it more likely had to do with the family name Moreau.

Morrilton: The seat of Conway County was originally Lewisburg, a ferry landing on the Arkansas River. In the 1870s, the Little Rock and Fort Smith Railroad built its line a mile distant from the town, and so residents relocated the town to the tracks. The businesses that grew up by the railroad took a name for landowners E.J. and George Morrill, who had sold the land to the railroad.

Napoleon (Desha): This once-important river port, which was the site of a federal marine hospital, was established around 1800 and named for the French emperor. Unfortunately, it flooded regularly, and since a particularly disastrous flood in 1874, its remains are now visible on sandbars only when the Mississippi is very low.

Nathan (Pike): Established in the mid-nineteenth century by Pleasant White and named for White's son-in-law, Nathan Lee Jones.

Neuhardt (Crittenden): Established as a lumber town around 1900 and named for landowner George Neuhardt. Alas, Neuhardt went bankrupt because of flooding and killed himself.

Newton County: Named for Thomas Willougby Newton, a member of the U.S. House of Representatives.

Norman (Montgomery): The settlement was first called Chivestown because of a Mr. Chives who ran a gristmill in the nineteenth century. All too briefly, the town was known as Pore Horse, allegedly because a local teacher commuted to work via horse and buggy and left the animal standing in harness all day. A more organized town was laid out in 1907 by land speculator Walter E. Womble Sr. at the railhead of the Gordon & Fort Smith Railroad and duly called Womble until 1925. Then the residents successfully changed the name to honor a Mrs. Norman from Oklahoma whose donation helped construct the Caddo Valley Academy. Womble, feeling unappreciated, thereupon moved to Fort Smith. One resident developed a neighborhood where he thought the railroad would come through and called it, for reasons known only to him, East Black

Springs. When the railroad went elsewhere, the neighborhood took on the breathtakingly glorious name of Middlebuster, surely unique in America.

Norvell *NOR-vuhl* (Crittenden): A logging community formed south of Earle in the late nineteenth century, it was first called Brown for early settler Tom Brown. Since it was close to Earle, it soon became known as New Earle and finally and officially as Norvell, for town leader Dr. Ben Norvell Sr. Eventually, it was simply incorporated into and is now a neighborhood of Earle.

Ogden (Little River): M.W. Bates founded the settlement sometime after 1880, using the maiden name of his second wife.

Old Austin (Lonoke): The town of Sandersville, named for settler William Sanders, was settled around 1850 and, in 1855, renamed Oakland Grove. A bit later, it was renamed Austin, perhaps in honor of Stephen F. Austin, who had been a landowner in the area for several years in the 1830s before moving to Texas and immortality. When the railroad bypassed the town by a mile, residents uprooted themselves and reestablished Austin, while the mostly abandoned settlement became Old Austin.

Old Hickory (Conway): This settlement grew up in the second half of the nineteenth century. According to a tenuous local legend, a first proposed name for a post office was rejected as too long, whereupon a resident suggested naming it after the nearby hickory trees. Another far more likely tale is that of a visiting merchant's suggestion to name it after Andrew Jackson. Deane elaborates on the story by naming Colonel Anderson Gordon as the merchant.

Oppelo (Conway): The town was settled in the middle of the nineteenth century on land belonging to L.B. Opolow, getting its post office in 1867. The official spelling has varied over the years.

Pankey (Pulaski): One of several African American communities established around 1908 by developer Josephine Irvin Pankey; now a part of Little Rock.

Patterson (Woodruff): Established in the 1880s as a railroad crossing and named Martin's Junction for the construction engineer. The name was changed to Jelks for a local family, and the town was finally renamed to honor the memory of a locally prominent sheriff, legislator and merchant, Marshall Patterson.

Perry County: Named—as was the county seat—Perryville for War of 1812 naval hero Oliver Hazard Perry.

Perrytown (Hempstead): Perry Campbell built a truck stop on U.S. Highway 67 in 1955 and added other stores with time. The town that grew up around the truck stop incorporated, against Campbell's wishes, with a name honoring him.

Pfeiffer (Independence): Now vanished, this town was settled in the 1860s by the Pfeiffer family, who operated the quarry whence came much of the stone for the state capitol and other buildings around the country.

Phillips County: Named for Sylvanus Phillips, a member of the territorial legislature.

Piggott *PIG-uht*: One of the two seats of Clay County, the town was originally called Huston but later renamed for James A. Piggott, an early settler, physician and postmaster. It is famous as the home of Ernest Hemingway's first wife. The Drew County family says *PEYE-gut*.

Pike County: Named, as was Pike City in the county, for explorer Zebulon Pike.

Pindall (Searcy): Originally called Kilburn when it was established around 1900, the town changed its name in 1908 to avoid confusion with the similar-sounding Gilbert and honors then-governor X.O. Pindall.

Plumerville *PLUHM-uhr-vil* (Conway): This onetime stagecoach stop and later railroad depot was named for early landowner Samuel Plummer, but lost an *m* along the way.

Pottsville (Pope): Kirkbride Potts settled here around 1830, and over the centuries, the town has also been called Galla Creek and Pott's Station.

Prescott: The source of the name given to the seat of Nevada County in 1873 was apparently a W.H. Prescott, but who he was is surprisingly unclear.

One tale says that he was one of the four surveyors who laid out the seat of Nevada County. Deane, in a lovely but hopelessly unlikely story, says that two of the surveyors were from Massachusetts and named the town for state historian William H. Prescott, who had died four years earlier. And Allsopp says that Prescott was an early county judge, a story so mundane that it is likely true.

Quitman (Cleburne and Faulkner Counties): Settled in the early nineteenth century and called Red River Mission, but when the post office was established in 1848, the town was named for Mexican War general John A. Quitman of Mississippi.

Randolph County: Named for John Randolph of Roanoke, a U.S. congressman from Virginia.

Rector (Clay): Established in 1882 as a station along the St. Louis and Texas Railroad and named for former governor Henry Massie Rector.

Reyno *REE-noh* (Randolph): The settlement was originally called Needmore, then Cherokee Bay and finally named for an early settler, Dennis Wells Reynolds. There are no known records explaining when and why the name was shortened.

Ruddell Hill (Independence): Founded early in the nineteenth century and first called Dry Run Creek, the settlement was later named for two of the original residents, brothers Abraham and George Ruddell. The town was annexed by Batesville in 1947.

Rudy (Crawford): A small settlement was established before the Civil War and named Kenton. The St. Louis–San Francisco Railroad came through and put up a depot named for George Rudy, who owned the land and became the first postmaster.

Russell (White): Founded in the 1870s on the St. Louis and Iron Mountain Railroad as a depot and named either by employee Russell Kaufman or, as Deane thinks, for an Irish construction worker, W.T. Russell, beloved for his sense of humor. The name was changed in 1878 to Plants but back to Russell in 1878.

Russellville: The seat of Pope County was settled in the 1830s and originally called Chactas Prairie, the Prairie and even Cactus Flats. In the 1840s, the residents voted for finally giving the town an official name, and the choice came down to honoring either store owner Jacob L. Shinn or Dr. Thomas Russell, an early settler. While Russell won the vote, some disgruntled residents insisted on calling the town Shinnville for a while.

Saffell *SAF-uhl* (Lawrence): Established in the first half of the nineteenth century and originally called Reeds Creek, the town was later renamed for a Confederate soldier and successful merchant, John Anderson Saffell.

Salesville (Baxter): Settled by John Sales after the Civil War and called either Sales or Spencer. The post office, which operated from 1941 to 1953, was called Ellis, but in 1968, the residents voted to incorporate it as Salesville.

Scott County: Named for Andrew Scott, a judge on the Arkansas Territory supreme court.

Scott (Pulaski and Lonoke Counties): Originally a railroad depot, it was first called Scott's Station and Scott's Crossing, and the name was eventually shortened. Conway Scott was the farmer whose land the railroad crossed and who had fought in court to stop the tracks, so the name was a sop to Cerberus.

Scottsville (Pope): The 1874 post office application was named for the Scott family, early settlers, but the town had previously been called Rocky Point, the Level and the Levey.

Searcy, county and city *SUHR-si*: The county was established in 1835 and named for Richard Searcy, a prominent citizen of Arkansas. In 1836, the county's name was changed to Marion for Francis Marion, and in 1838, the southern half of the county was made into a new county with the original name of Searcy. The town of Searcy is, naturally, the seat of White County. First called Frankfurt, its name was changed in 1838 to honor the same Richard Searcy.

Sheridan: Seat, appropriately, of Grant County, settled after the Civil War, and named for the ferocious Union cavalry lieutenant general Philip Sheridan.

Sherrill (Jefferson): A railroad depot that developed into a town and was first named Barrett for landowner John M. Barrett. Since the railroad had another station in Texas named Barrett, the station was renamed, apparently in honor of local physician A.R. Sherrill, stepfather of John.

Shover Springs (Hempstead): The medicinal waters of the springs have long been famous. The settlement was named for local merchant George W. Shover and at times also called Shover's Spring and Shover's Springs.

Sidney (Sharp): Settled in the 1840s but not given a post office until 1878. The postmaster apparently named it to honor Albert Sidney Johnston, his commander during the Civil War. Johnston died at Shiloh, as did the postmaster's son.

Skull Creek (Washington): Deane says that the settlement was named for U.S. Army chaplain William Scull, who was preaching in the area around 1840, and the spelling later and unfortunately changed.

Spielerville (Logan): Formerly a relay station on the Military Road named Creole. There is evidence that it was perhaps settled by Louisianans. Around 1888, the name was changed to honor brothers Emil and Louis Spieler. The 1909 depot at Subiaco, just a mile away, led to the town's decline, and it was gone by 1930.

Stamps (Lafayette): Established after 1870 around a lumber mill owned by Hardy James Stamps. Prosperity came with the Louisiana & Arkansas Railroad, and the first post office, in 1888, was named for Stamps.

Stella (Izard): Settled in the mid-nineteenth century, originally called Bone Town after the Bone family of pioneers. The name was changed in 1897 for a five-year old girl, Stella Davidson. The town eventually became part of Mount Pleasant.

Swifton (Jackson): The settlement, largely on land belonging to the Swift family, was established in the 1870s as a sawmill and then a depot on the Cairo and Fulton Railroad.

Tokio (Hempstead): The town is on the Tokio sand formation, but Deane attributes the name to early resident Tokio Huddleston. Whether the name is owing to a distinctive personal name or an obscure geological term is not a common question in historical toponymy.

Tollette *TAHL-uht* (Howard): This town has a variety of competing explanations for its name, including one about a community of freed slaves who gathered there in the 1870s, led by Sanford Jackson Washington Tollette. Another history says that the town had been settled by the middle of the nineteenth century and originally called Blackland Township but the 1891 post office was named for postmaster Sanford J.W. Tollette. A third and unlikely tale says that the 1891 attempt to get a post office named Toltec was denied, and the name was made Tollette.

Tomberlin (Lonoke): Settled around 1880, this town was formed around a store owned by James E. Tomberlin and so was originally—and sometimes still is—called Tomberlins.

Treat (Pope): Deane says that it was named for early settler "Uncle Polk" Treat.

Tull (Grant County and Saline): Both towns were settled in the mid-nineteenth century and named for prominent local families. The Saline town was called Belfast when it was settled in 1854, and after 1887, it was named for John M. Tull, the first postmaster.

Van Buren: The seat of Crawford County was a busy port on the Arkansas River before the Civil War and originally called Phillips Landing. In 1831, it was renamed for then secretary of state Martin Van Buren.

Waldron: The seat of Scott County was established in the 1830s and named Poteau Valley, until the brother of the town's founder and postmaster, W.G. Featherston, essentially took away the post office in 1845 and moved it to a new location, which he named Winfield. Featherston had the town replatted and named for the surveyor W.P. Waldron, who platted it.

Warren: The Bradley County seat was settled in the 1830s, and its early names included Cabeens, Saline Settlement and Pennington Settlement. According to tradition, it was finally named for a slave freed by settler Hugh Bradley. Deane notes that in his will, Bradley left Warren, an enslaved person, to his wife, but Allsopp says that Warren was enslaved by Bradley's son-in-law. A more likely possibility is that it was named for Bradley's close friend Edward Allen Warren, a lawyer in Camden.

Washburn (Sebastian): Established in the 1870s, the town was named, according to Deane, for missionary Cephas Washburn, who had established the Dwight Mission around 1820 and was the father of painter Edward Payson Washburn.

Wheatley (St. Francis): A depot on the Memphis and Little Rock Railroad, established around 1870 and first called Britton, then renamed for local resident Wheatley Dennis.

White County: There are no known records of the origin of this county's name. Some say the county was named for the White River, others that it was named for Hugh L. White, a U.S. senator from Tennessee. Deane holds with the latter, telling those favoring the river theory, "The evidence indicates otherwise," but he doesn't specify what evidence.

Widener *WIDE-nuhr* (St. Francis): A depot established in 1888 on the Memphis & Little Rock Railroad, originally called Mead for the local postmaster, then renamed to honor regional farmer and lumberman John M. Widener.

Wiederkehr Village (Franklin): Reputed to be the smallest city in Arkansas, it was settled in 1881 by Johann Andreas Wiederkehr, who came from Switzerland and soon established vineyards and a winery.

Williams Junction (Perry): The settlement was named after the death of founders Pink and Louise Williams.

Withrow Springs State Park (Madison): Farmer and miller T.J. Withrow gave his name to the springs and, eventually, the park.

Woodruff County: Named for William Woodruff, the first newspaper publisher in Arkansas.

Woodson (Pulaski): Developed after the Civil War, the town was first called Pennington's Mills. In 1871, when a railroad depot was built, it was renamed Campbell for a local judge, and in 1881, it got its current name.

A local story says that it is named for Ed Wood Sr., a local landowner and/or the first African American plantation owner in Arkansas, but there is no proof for this. More likely, it bears the name of a local family who owned many acres.

Wynne: The seat of Cross County was established along the St. Louis, Iron Mountain and Southern Railroad at the spot where a train had derailed. An abandoned boxcar became Wynne Station, named for Texas Civil War soldier and Forrest City banker Jesse Watkins Wynne, and the town grew up around it.

Yell County: Named for Archibald Yell, the second governor of Arkansas.

Yellville: The seat of Marion County was established in the early nineteenth century and originally called Shawneetown because early residents used buildings constructed by recently—and forcibly—departed Shawnee Indians. When the county was created in 1836, the residents chose to rename the town after Archibald Yell.

Yell County Courthouse. *Courtesy Brandonrush. Own work, CC BY-SA 3.0, https://commons. wikimedia.org/w/index.php?curid=27983809.*

Yoestown (Crawford): Plantation owner Jacob Yoes, who had served as a colonel in the Union army, owned much land in the area.

Yorktown (Lincoln): When it was settled in the mid-nineteenth century, the town was named not for the Virginia site but for the York family.

Zack (Searcy): Originally named Kimbell Springs for an early settler, a Unionist whose son was lynched during the Civil War, it became a station on the Missouri & North Arkansas Railroad and, in 1903, was renamed for local landowner Zack Johnson. It was also the home of musician and presidential candidate James Elton Baker, a.k.a. Elton Britt.

Chapter 3

NATURAL FEATURES

The same natural barriers that frustrated early settlement also provided the settlers with names as they built their towns next to rivers, between hills or amid forests. Many of the rivers and bayous were navigable far into the land, and landmarks along the waterways allowed travelers to know their position by, say, notable pines along a bluff, a remarkable grouping of small rocks or a natural dam across the river. As settlement moved inland, mountains and valleys took on descriptive names.

The abundance of flora and fauna, also, is clear from many place names. Settlers noted the pea vines, the flowers and especially the trees, a ready source of lumber and fuel. Among the wildlife that intrigued (and fed) early settlers, bison and bears were appreciated and wolves and cougars were feared, while turkeys, parakeets and many other less controversial animals found their way onto the Arkansas map.

Alpine (Clark): Settled in the 1840s and perhaps—and imaginatively—named for being the highest point in the county. Other tales suggest the influence of an early family named McAlpine, but the best—if most doubtful—story involves a pine tree behind the post office in which an owl roosted and so was called the Owl Pine.

Appleton (Pope): According to town legend, the original 1879 post office was in a drugstore surrounded by an apple orchard.

Arlberg, town and rock formation, Arlberg Arch (Stone): Settled as a railroad camp after 1900 and first known as Red River or Lexington. The name may be a railway worker's, or perhaps it was given by someone comparing the scenery to that along the Arlberg Railway in the Austrian Alps.

Ash Flat: Settled in 1856, the county seat of Sharp County is said to have been named for a nearby grove of ash trees on level ground where the town was built.

Bald Knob (White): In the nineteenth century, a bald was a field of tall grasses and shrubs, a definition carried to Arkansas by settlers from the Appalachians. This particular bald was named for a large outcropping of stone, especially visible from the White River. It was possibly the site of the Native American village Palisima, mentioned in documents from the Hernando de Soto expedition. The elevation remained dry in the midst of marshes and even during the 1927 flood. A good, if not particularly accurate, story was told by gubernatorial candidate Earl Hodges, who said that it was named for his opponent, Charles H. Brough.

Bass (Newton): The post office began in 1902 and was named because of the many bass to be found in (and pulled from) Big Creek.

Bay (Craighead): Settled in the 1870s, but a town only began to grow when the railroad came through. A siding was called Bay Siding, owing to the large slough nearby known as Big Bay. The first post office was called Big Bay, then the name was shortened to Bay.

Bayou *BYE-oh*: The origin of this commonly used word has led to much disagreement among scholars. The standard explanation is that because Choctaw was the lingua franca of early traders and Indians, the Choctaw word *bayuk*, meaning "a sluggish or stagnant water course," took on widespread use, even in the upstate, where it is a marker of French ethnicity. Some, on the other hand, say that the word derives from French *bayouc*, "a stream of dead water," or perhaps from *boyau*, meaning "gut or narrow passage," and that *bayuk*, in Creek, simply means "creek" or "river."

Bear, mountain and town (Garland): This boomtown of the 1880s was named for the mountain, which was named for the number of bears in the area.

Bellefonte *BELL-font* (Boone): Settled just before the Civil War with a productive spring of fresh water and named, as the story goes, by residents who thought that the name was Latin for "beautiful spring."

Big Flat: Straddling the Baxter and Searcy county line and named for a plateau in the Ozark Mountains near Big Creek, since *flat* was an Appalachian word for the top of a ridge. One story says that the town was first called Big Yellow Flat.

Black Fork town and mountain (Scott): Both named for the Black Fork Creek which was so named for its dark water.

Black Oak: There are three of these towns in Arkansas. The one in Craighead County was settled in the late nineteenth century as a timber town and perhaps first called Kimbrell. The 1902 post office was called Dwight, after local Baptist minister Dwight Hall. At the same time, a nearby railroad station was named Black Oak because it was on Black Oak Ridge, and that name has stuck and become famous thanks to the rock band Black Oak Arkansas.

Black Springs (Montgomery): Established in the mid-nineteenth century and named for either the black rocks—possibly manganese ore or iron ore—or else for a Black family that may or may not have lived there at some point.

Boat Mountain (Boone): Allegedly so named because someone thought the mountain looked like a boat.

Bodock: This is the name of several creeks in southern Arkansas, probably derived from *bois d'arc*, the Osage orange, so called because the Caddos made and traded bows made from the wood of this tree.

Boeuf River (Chicot): A 1784 report called it La Riviere aux Boeufs, referring to bison.

Boiling Springs (Pope): Deane recounts a tale that, in the 1830s, it was so named by a Methodist pastor because he thought the water came boiling out of the springs.

Bozarth (Benton): Deane speculates that this is another mutation of *bois d'arc*.

Bruin (Crittenden): A hunting reserve south of Horseshoe Lake, established by St. Louis manufacturer Russell Gardner and named for the bears in the area.

Buffalo City (Baxter) Located where the Buffalo River empties into the White River, probably as far upstream as paddle wheelers could go. The town straddles the White River, with Old Buffalo City on the western side and New on the east bank.

Buffalo River: The first National River Monument in America, named for the herds of bison that once roamed its banks.

Bull Shoals (Marion): Developed after World War II to be a planned community on the shore of the lake created by the new Bull Shoals Dam. The shoals along the White River take their name from the French *boill*, meaning "a large spring." Deane recounts a tale of Tennessean Edmund Jenkins, who lived in the area in the late eighteenth century and told of six large springs, or "boils," which he called "bulls." But Deane also notes an unlikely story of an Indian family named Bull.

Calico Rock (Izard): Established as a steamboat landing on the White River and named for the bluffs on the north bank, whose strips of blue, black, gray, red and orange rock face gave the appearance of calico cloth.

Cane Hill (Washington): Settled in 1827, and the first post office (1830) was Cane Hill, because it was built on a large hill covered with cane. In 1839, the town became Steam Mill, and in 1843, resident Major William Boone, related to Daniel Boone, had the town renamed Boonsborough or Boonsboro, presumably for Daniel. Cane Hill College was organized in 1834, and the town was the site of the 1862 Civil War Battle of Cane Hill. One precious story says that the town was at one time called Hillsboro for "a much-respected old lady, Mrs. Viney Hill," surely the best story of the lot.

Cave City (Sharp and Independence Counties): Settled in the late nineteenth century and named for the Crystal River Cave beneath the city. The cave was first called Horn's Cave, for early settler Henry Horn. While the cave initially had a sinister reputation, townspeople began to suggest that the water had healing properties. The city now incorporates

Cedar Grove and Loyal, the latter allegedly so named because the founder remained loyal to the Union during the Civil War.

Cave Springs (Benton): A small settlement developed around the middle of the nineteenth century and originally named Cannon for one of the settlers, a Mr. Fincannon. When the Kansas City & Memphis Railroad came through, the area was renamed for its two caves and the large spring flowing from one of them.

Cedar Creek (Scott): Established in 1852 were two towns about three miles apart, Little Cedar and Big Cedar, each on the bank of that particular tributary of the Fourche La Fave. Eventually, residents just began calling the area Cedar Creek.

Cedar Grove (Independence): Settled after the middle of the nineteenth century and grew significantly after the Civil War. In 1899, the USPS refused to allow the name Cedar Grove, since another Cedar Grove was just twenty miles away. The Post Office approved Alonzo, one of the names of town postmaster Joel Asa Alonzo "Tobe" Pearson, from the three choices submitted by the town. That post office closed around 1918 and the town soon disappeared.

Cedarville (Crawford): Established in 1870 as Spencer's Shop and renamed Cedarville in 1872, presumably because there were more cedar trees than Spencers.

Chalybeate Springs *KLEE-bit* (Stone): Settled after the Civil War and originally called Bon Air Spring, the town later took on this complicated name based on an archaic term for "salts of iron."

Cherry Valley (Cross): Established in the 1860s and named for a grove of cherry trees between two hogback ridges or for some cherry trees growing along Cooper's Creek. Or maybe both.

Chimney Rock (Madison): Named for its shape.

Clifty (Madison): The birthplace of baseball star Arky Vaughan, the town was named, according to Deane in one of his especially curious tales, for the many local cliffs.

Clover Bend (Lawrence): Settled as a steamship landing in the 1820s, it was so named for all the bends in the Black River. In the 1930s, it was reestablished as one of many communities in the United States dedicated to helping small farmers become independent.

Cricket (Boone): Settled near a railroad tunnel project in the early 1900s along Cricket Creek, which Deane says was probably named on account of the insects.

Daisy, town and state park (Pike): The town was established in the late nineteenth century and first called Gentry, but to avoid confusion with that town in Benton County, the postmistress, Churbry Meeks, reportedly named the town for a field of wild daisies near the post office.

Delaplaine (Greene): Possibly the site of Indian villages and later a French trading post called De La Plaine on account of its height above the local wetlands. The post office combined all three words into one.

DeRoche Creek and Town *dee-ROHCH* (Hot Spring): DeRoche Creek appears on an 1806 map, and Hunter calls the stream Bayu des Roches, "Bayou of the Rocks." There is a story about a German settler named Holstein giving it that name, which seems improbable.

Eglantine (Van Buren): The town's post office was established in 1866, and the reasonable assumption is that the town was named for the wild pink roses that grew abundantly on the hillsides.

El Paso (White): Begun in the early nineteenth century in the valley between Cadron Ridge and Bull Mountain and named for "the pass." The first post office in 1850 was called Olive Creek and was renamed El Paso in 1869.

Elm Springs (Washington and Benton Counties): The town, which was settled in the 1830s and grew up around the Elm Springs Methodist Episcopal Church, followed the church's lead in commemorating both a grove of elms and the natural water springs that powered a mill.

Fallsville (Newton): When the town was established in 1883, the postmaster, a Mr. Dixon, explained that he wanted a name descriptive of the surrounding terrain.

Ferndale (Pulaski): Ferns growing around a nearby spring were the inspiration for the 1914 name chosen by the town, which developed around 1900.

Fountain Hill (Ashley): Established in the mid-nineteenth century, with two springs on either side of a hill.

Fountain Lake (Garland): The town developed after World War II around a resort built circa 1920, on a lake made by a dammed-up creek. A fountain in the middle of the resort's swimming pool gave the resort its name.

Grapevine (Grant): The town was settled in the 1880s and named for a legendary grapevine that covered a huge swath of land. A twelve-foot cutting required six men to carry it, and a photograph of the event was long displayed in the post office. Deane relates settlers' memories of having to hack their way through other enormous vines to make the road from Sheridan and Rison.

Gravel Hill (Saline): Established around 1900 as African American families formed a community that they named for the rocky soil. The name changed to Southside Community and, in 2002, to Ralph Bunche Community.

Gravel Ridge (Pulaski): Settlers in the early nineteenth century named their town for the loose stones on the high ground. Interestingly, when a Baptist Church formed in 1892, all its original members came over from Flint Hills Baptist Church.

Grapevine. *Author's collection.*

Gravelly (Yell): The post office at Gravelly Hill was established in 1871, but the "Hill" was dropped from common use almost immediately. The story is that a singularly unimaginative early settler exclaimed, "What a gravelly place!" and the name stuck.

Greenbrier (Faulkner): Established in the middle of the nineteenth century and first called Mooresville, it soon took its current name from nearby Greenbrier Creek, so called for the plentiful saw brier.

Green Forest (Carroll): The birthplace of Helen Gurley Brown was established after the Civil War. The only story about its name is implausible: the postmaster, John Grim, in clearing his farmland, left a grove of trees, which was dubbed by neighbors the Green Forest.

Greenhill (Drew): This small community in western Drew County is served by two churches, each of which spells the town's name differently: the Greenhill Baptist Church and the Green Hill Methodist Church. And there are two stories: one credits a family's large acreage, which included a hill that turned green in early spring, although the story does not say how that in any way distinguished it from any other hill in southern Arkansas. The more pedestrian tale says that early settlers included a Green family, although any trace of their presence is gone.

Gum Springs (Clark): Settled in the early nineteenth century and probably named for a spring, popularly used for swimming and baptizing, at the base of a sweetgum tree.

Variant spellings of Greenhill. *Author's collection.*

Hickory Ridge (Cross): The original name of this town was the wonderful Spice Swamps, but with the 1875 post office came the more respectable Hickory Ridge, appropriate only in that there may have been hickory trees, but there is certainly no ridge in this part of the delta.

Highland (Sharp): A small town, presumably named for the geography, struggled (and failed) to survive in the late nineteenth century. Locating a high school there in 1962 revived the town's fortunes.

Holly Grove (Monroe): A plantation community established in 1836 and named for thickets of holly trees.

Hollywood: The early seat of Clark County was founded in the early nineteenth century and first called Greenville. In the 1850s, the name changed to Anvil, and in 1860, it became Holly Wood. Eventually, it became one word. The post office closed in 1954.

Horseshoe Bend (Izard): Developed as a retirement community in the 1970s and named for a feature of the Strawberry River.

Horseshoe Lake (Crittenden) A settlement of the late nineteenth century was originally called Seyppel but is now named for the oxbow lake.

Hot Spring County: Named for the naturally occurring hot springs within the county when it was formed and which are now, after the county lines were redrawn, located in the newer Garland County.

Hot Springs: The county seat of Garland—and not, as one might guess, of Hot Spring County—is named for the famous thermal springs. The town was first so called on a map in 1818, and in 1832, the U.S. Congress created the Hot Springs Reservation.

Lake City: One of two seats of Craighead County, but near no known lake! Settled in the 1830s as a landing on the St. Francis River, it was first called Old Town. But because there was another Old Town, the 1878 post office name was Sunk Lands. In 1886, it became Lake City because the river was very wide at that point, although later dredging has made the river narrow and the "lake" a faded memory.

Lake View (Phillips): The Farm Security Administration established this town north of Old Town Lake in 1937 as one of the three communities in Arkansas reserved for African American farming families. The name was spelled as both one word and two until 1980, when the town was incorporated.

Lake Village: The seat of Chicot County and named for its location on Lake Chicot.

Little River County: Named for the Little River, which flows into the Red River. This is distinct from the Little River in northeastern Arkansas, but there are no records of how either got its name.

Little Rock: The capital of Arkansas and seat of Pulaski County was named for a small rock formation on the south bank of the Arkansas River. French explorers called this landmark for river traffic La Petite Roche. These rocks had been noted in early eighteenth-century documents, but the designation first showed up on a map in 1799. The first settlement was in 1820, and the post office that year was called Little Rock. Deane has no patience with the legend of Bernard de La Harpe giving the rock its name, although La Harpe is on record as sighting Le Rocher Francais, the tall bluff on the other bank of the Arkansas. Deane mentions a land deed of 1814, of disputed authenticity, referring to "little rocks bluff." In 1826, a group holding New Madrid certificates attempted to claim ownership and rename the town Arkopolis, but their claims were not upheld in court, and the name endures.

Locust Bayou (Calhoun): Named by the French Bayu Accacia for the locust trees and simply translated into English.

Locust Grove (Independence): Founded in the 1830s and named for locust trees nearby.

Lone Pine (Johnson): Early settlers from Tennessee named their settlement for a large pine tree near the church.

Lonoke *LOH-noke* (Lonoke): The city, from which the county takes its name, was established as a railroad depot in 1868. One story says that two railroad contractors, Rumbough and Robinson, named it for three groups of large red oaks. One of the contractors wonderfully suggested a spelling that would give it a vaguely Native American sound, Lo-no-kah, but that pronunciation never caught on. A more likely—and also interesting—tale is that the contractors named the station for a large red oak tree that stood isolated on the prairie, where the county courthouse now stands, and was used as a landmark. They spelled it Lone Oak, pronounced *low-NOKE*, but a newspaper misprint changed it to Lonoak, and eventually the spelling and pronunciation were further mangled to the current form.

Magnet Cove (Hot Spring): The community, formed in the nineteenth century, was named for the geological shape of the ground and the abundance of magnetite or lodestone, which was attracted to the plows and other tools of early settlers.

Mammoth Spring, state park and town in Fulton County: A settlement grew up around the large spring, originally called Head of the River. The name was most likely changed to attract tourists.

Marble Falls (Newton): Originally called Marble City on account of the nearby quarry. Although it was a small quarry, a block taken from there was sent to the national capital and is part of the Washington Monument. In 1883, the town of Wilcockson, named for the first postmaster, was officially established, but the residents continued to call it Marble City and then Marble Falls. The "falls" part of the name was from a small waterfall nearby, where there had been a gristmill. From 1968 to 1997, seeking commercial glory, the town changed its name to Dogpatch, in order to promote that unfortunate amusement park. After the park closed, the earlier name was restored.

Mineral Springs (Howard): Settled in the nineteenth century and first called Saline. By mid-century, it was popularly known as Greenville, although the post office name remained Saline. In 1869, the town was renamed by local boosters for its springs, which were proclaimed not only medicinal but also the best and purest water in Arkansas.

Mount Holly (Union): The town grew up around an 1845 Presbyterian church, and the residents were impressed by the remarkable number of holly trees growing on a nearby hillside.

Mountainburg (Crawford): What became a town was originally a stop on the Butterfield Overland Mail Company route and later a depot for the St. Louis–San Francisco Railway. One local history ventures the curious belief that the name is owing to "its location at the foothills of the Boston Mountains."

Mountain Pine (Garland): The Dierks Lumber Company purchased land near Hawes in 1922 and laid out a company town in 1926, the name celebrating its location in the Ouachita Mountains.

Mountain Top (Franklin): Named appropriately, if not imaginatively, because the post office was in fact on the top of an Ozark mountain.

Mountain View: The seat of Stone County since the formation of the county in 1873. The name was picked, after some intense disagreement, by a drawing. Given its location in the Ozarks, it's easy to understand the origin.

Muddy Fork (Howard): Local history notes only that the town was formed inside a bend of Muddy Fork Creek, which begs the question of where the creek got its name.

Mulberry (Crawford): A creek and town named for the many mulberry trees along the stream.

Natural Dam (Crawford): Limestone rocks, piled eight feet thick in places, partially blocked Mountain Fork Creek and prompted early settlers to name the feature.

Natural Steps (Pulaski): The town was established in the last half of the nineteenth century and named for a nearby sandstone formation that looks like parallel stair steps up the mountainside.

Norfork (Baxter): Established as the seat of Izard County early in the nineteenth century on the junction of the White and North Fork Rivers. The town's name was Izard Court House from 1824 until 1844, when it officially became North Fork, but it was more popularly called Liberty. In 1902, there was a movement, apparently led by construction workers building a railroad bridge over the White River, to call the town Devero, to honor a popular French railroad engineer, Devereaux. But the movement petered out, and in 1906, the post office took on the town's current name, now shortened to a single word.

Oak Bower (Hot Spring): A town near Bismarck was settled in the latter half of the nineteenth century, apparently in the midst of many oaks.

Oak Grove Heights (Greene): When the Methodists settled here in the 1870s, it became one of several towns called Oak Grove. The Iron Mountain Railroad constructed a depot nearby with the interesting name of Knoxburn, for the nearby Knox-Woodburn dairy farm. In 1938, the town finally incorporated and attempted to distinguish itself from the other Oak Groves while eschewing the more interesting Knoxburn.

Oakland (Marion): Established in the late nineteenth century and marvelously called Orcutt Flat. Around 1900, the name was changed, probably because of all the trees.

Overcup, lake and town (Conway): Probably both are named for overcup oak trees.

Ozone (Johnson): Settled in the mid-nineteenth century. Local history records that postmistress Delia McCracken, in 1875, picked the name using the contemporary meaning of *ozone*: "the fresh and distinctive smell in the atmosphere following a thunderstorm." There is no word on how the town smelled the rest of the time.

Pansy (Cleveland): First called Bradley when it was settled after the Civil War. In 1881, it was renamed, for reasons unknown, for the flower.

Panther Creek (Newton): Legend says that it was so named because a settler named Hudson killed a cougar on the creek bank.

Paroquet *pair-uh-KEET* (Independence): Settled in the early nineteenth century and called Berkley, then renamed for the Carolina parakeet, using the older spelling of the word. Since farmers regarded parakeets as pests, it is unclear why a town would be named for the bird.

Pea Ridge (Benton and Desha Counties): Pea Ridge in Benton County was settled early in the nineteenth century and named for the abundance of wild peas that grew on the hillside. When the post office was established in 1850, the name was one word, but eventually, it separated into two. Deane notes that Federal accounts of the Civil War battle sometimes call it Peavine Ridge.

Similarly, in Desha County, whippoorwill peas were grown in abundance on a local ridge.

Penter's Bluff (Izard): Deane collected three distinct tales for this name. In the first, we have two Penter brothers dueling for the hand of a girl, although the bluff is named for only one Penter. The second is the story of a young schoolteacher, Susan Penter, who had her horse stolen by Yankees but later recovered it—another lovely but improbable tale. Simpler and far more likely is the third explanation of Deane's: that *penter* was a local pronunciation of "panther."

Pine Bluff: The seat of Jefferson County was settled in the 1820s on a high bank of the Arkansas River marked by some tall pine trees. Originally called Mount Maria, by 1832, it was known more simply as Pine Bluff Town.

Pine Ridge (Montgomery): The 1930s radio show *Lum and Abner* was set in fictional Pine Ridge but based on the town of Waters, which was established in 1886 and named for its founder, Henry M. Waters. To cash in on the show's media fame, the town changed its name in 1936.

Pineville (Izard): Settled in the middle of the nineteenth century and named accurately, if unimaginatively, for the many pine trees. The name was changed in 1920 to Whit, for postmaster Whit Young, and then, for reasons unrecorded, back to Pineville in 1922.

Pinnacle Mountain (Pulaski): Known in the early nineteenth century as Maumelle Mountain but later allegedly referred to as "that pinnacle." Now it is part of a state park, and a nearby community has taken on the name.

Plainview (Yell): A ferry crossing of the Petit Jean River was first called Ward, for the two landowners with that name, and then—delightfully—Balloon or Balloun in 1879. When the Ward's Crossing Bridge over the Fourche La Fave River was completed in 1905, prosperity came to the town, along with a new name, in 1907. Deane has one of the early settlers exclaiming, "What a plain view." This prosaic story has acquired details, and eventually the settler was identified as Mrs. W.W. Gardner, who, with her husband, ran the mill in the center of town and who is supposed to have said that the mill offered a plain view of the area. Altogether, a change for the worse.

Pleasant Grove (Stone): Probably because of the iron ore in the soil, the town was originally called Red Stripe. Bad publicity from a 1929 rape and murder case led to what the residents hoped would be a more cheerful name.

Pleasant Plains (Independence): Established in the early nineteenth century on the Southwest Trail and originally called Fairview. When the 1842 application for a post office with that name was rejected, the residents settled for the current name.

Point Cedar, creek and town (Hot Spring): Established in the 1850s, the settlement was named Cedar Point for the trees where the creek joins the Caddo River. The USPS said there was already another Cedar Point, so the name was simply reversed.

Poke Bayou: The bayou flows from Sharp County into the White River and was possibly named for the pokeberry, although there is a claim that *poke* was another word for the green heron. Several settlements have had this name, including Batesville. A town by this name in Sharp County, which was abandoned in 1914, was first called Martin's Store, since the post office was in John Martin's store, and that name is preserved in that of the historic site. Some locals claim that the town was, in fact, called Polk Bayou—and the name was changed to Polk in 1894.

Possum Grape (Jackson): In the early nineteenth century, there was a busy port and ferry on the White River at Grand Glaise (also spelled Glaize or Glaze). When the Cairo and Fulton Railroad bypassed the town in the 1870s, most residents relocated to the railroad and, in 1954, came up with this marvelous name, which comes from the wild grape. Some say—with more imagination than evidence—that an argument in 1954 over whether to call the town Possum or Grape led to the combination.

Possum Grape. *Courtesy of OzarksRazorback. Own work, CC BY-SA 4.0, https://commons.wikimedia.org/w/index.php?curid=42163438.*

Possum Valley. *Courtesy of Kay Craig Spurlock.*

Possum Run (Baxter): The road was allegedly so named because it was a trail heavily used by possums at night.

Possum Trost (Conway): Allsopp says this should be Tryst—where opossums would gather in persimmon trees—and he cites a unique expression from the area, "Live 'possums and persimmons, dead 'possum and 'taters."

Possum Valley (Drew): There are four or five tales, gaining details with each retelling, that all involve hunters getting lost in the woods and having (or refusing) to eat unsalted opossum to survive.

Potato Hill Mountain (Yell): Deane says that it was so named because of its resemblance to a potato hill; in fact, there are several Potato Hills around Arkansas.

Prairie County: Named for the Grand Prairie of eastern Arkansas. Settlers used the word *prairie* to describe open, grassy areas that were burned by the Indigenous peoples to drive game. These prairies were far different from the flat expanses in the delta.

Prairie Grove (Drew): A station on the Ashley, Drew & Northern Railroad in the early 1900s was named for a small grove of trees on an otherwise flat grassland. Oddly, the post office, while it existed, was called Scipio.

Prairie Grove (Washington): Settled around 1830, the town was originally called Sweet Home, and in 1857, it became Ada, named for one of the postmaster's daughters. There are no records of how or why the third and final name came about, but it was in time for the bloody Civil War battle of Prairie Grove.

Ravenden Springs (Randolph): Settled after 1880. Deane recounts the tale of a minister's dream in which his stomach ailment was cured by water from the mountain. He traveled there and was healed, and the springs gained a reputation as miraculous, while the settlement called itself Dream Town. It later was renamed to incorporate reference to the springs. Local history says that there was a great nest of ravens up in a canyon, but in fact, a storied nest and colony had been gone for at least twenty years.

Red River: Deane reports early records of it being called Negite or Nigitai, meaning "red" in some Indian language. Early maps show it as Riviere Rouge or Rothe, and it was similarly called by the Spanish Rio Colorado or Rio Vermejo.

Rockport (Hot Spring): Large boulders in the Ouachita River made this a good place to ford the river, and so a settlement grew up there in the early nineteenth century. The post office with this name opened in 1837, and the town served as the county seat from 1846 until 1879.

Rose Bud (White): Settled just before the Civil War and allegedly named in 1858 by Louise Hill, sister of the postmaster, because of a rosebush in her yard.

Rush (Marion): The now-vanished former site of a zinc mine was allegedly named because of the disastrous floods from the creek.

Sage (Izard): Local lore says that the post office, established in 1887, was so named on account of the abundance of tall sage grass in the area.

Saline County *suh-LEEN*: One of the first counties in Arkansas, it was named for the salt reserves found within its borders. The Saline River may be so named for the same salt reserves, or perhaps for the salty marsh where it flows into the Ouachita River, called by the early French settlers the Marais Saline. Allsopp attributes the name to the number of buffalo salt licks in the area.

Shoal Creek: Deane notes that it was first called Rocky Creek because a nearby ledge could make the Arkansas River difficult to navigate at low water, but why its name was changed is not known.

Snow Lake (Desha): Dean says that a nearby lake, covered by water lilies, inspired the name.

Soda Bluff (Madison): Deane describes chalk from a cliff, so white that it looked like soda, that was used by settlers as a cleaning agent.

Springdale (Washington and Benton Counties): Site of a station on the Butterfield Overland Mail Company's route, established in the 1840s, the settlement was first called Holcombe Springs and then Shiloh, for a Primitive Baptist church. In 1872, the USPS would not allow Shiloh since there was another one in the state, so a settler suggested Springdale, short for "springs in the dale."

Springfield (Conway): Long a trading post at a crossroads with a reliable spring, the town was established in 1850 as the new county seat. Perhaps, as Allsopp surmises, the town grew up around a spring in a field.

Springtown (Benton): Settled after the Civil War and called Hickory until 1874, when the name was changed on account of the spring that is the source of Flint Creek.

Stone County: Named for the rocky ridges and rocky soil—and not, Deane is adamant, for a person.

Strawberry (Lawrence): John A. Cathey settled here in the 1870s and called the community Cathey. When the post office needed a name in 1881, he suggested to his neighbors calling it Cathey Town. The other residents balked, but he was successful with his second idea: naming it for the Strawberry River.

Strawberry River: Named for the wild berries that grew on its banks.

Sugarloaf Mountain and Lake (Sebastian): A common name for hills across America that resembled the loaves of molded sugar maple sap made by pioneers.

Sulphur Rock (Independence): Established early in the nineteenth century on the Old Military Road and named for the two sulfur springs nearby.

Sulphur Springs (Benton): Settled in the 1870s and named for the numerous natural springs, including a lithium spring.

Sulphur Springs (Jefferson): This was a mid-nineteenth-century site for resort hotels using local spring waters, but in 1855, the name was disallowed for the post office because of another Sulphur Springs. So the official name became White Sulphur Springs until the mid-twentieth century, when the "White" was dropped.

Terre Noire *TURN-war* or *TURN-wall* (Clark): The town that existed from 1846 to 1866 is gone, but the creek remains, named perhaps because it runs through black soil and thus gets its color. Similar to:

Terre Rouge Creek *tare-ROOZH* (Nevada and Clark), which is likewise said to get its red tint from having run through red soil.

Three Brothers (Baxter): The community was originally called Vin when it was settled in the late nineteenth century, but in 1900, the postmaster asked that the town be named for the three-humped mountain range nearby. There are several local legends about three specific brothers, but there is no evidence for any of the stories.

Tigre Creek *tigger* (Hot Spring): In early journals, the creek is called Fourche a Tigre, and there is evidence that in the regional French patois, *tigre* is "puma" or "panther."

Tumbling Shoals (Cleburne): The town and bridge were both named for the shoals in the Red River.

Tupelo (Jackson): Established in the mid-nineteenth century, the town, in 1884, got a post office wonderfully named Ibet. The name was changed that same year to Tupelo, either for the trees or for the name of the plantation of Micajah B. McCoy.

Turkey (Marion): Allsopp weakly offers that wild turkeys used to abound in the area.

Vache Grasse Creek (Sebastian): Deane speculates that the name came for bison either seen or killed along the creek.

Violet Hill (Izard): Local legend says that the town, settled in the mid-nineteenth century, was named for the wildflowers that grew in great number.

Waveland (Logan): Settled around 1870 by A.V. Reff, who became the first postmaster in 1881 and who chose the name because his daughter said that from Mount Magazine, it looked like the hills were waving at her.

Western Grove (Newton): Settled before the Civil War and first called Marshall Prairie, so named for the postmaster in 1854. In 1886, the name was changed, according to local history, in celebration of an especially lovely grove just to the west of the prairie.

West Fork (Washington): Two towns, dating back to the 1820s, grew up along the west fork of the White River. The second, which was first called Woolsey and then Pitkin, eventually was joined to the first, which had always been named for the river.

White River: The name is popularly attributed to the appearance of water, which, when compared to the Mississippi, is very clear. Indigenous names included Unica or Nika; on French maps it was La Riviere Blanche.

Wolf Bayou (Cleburne): Settled in the mid-nineteenth century on a creek (at the time called a bayou). For the 1851, post office application, the "Wolf" was added because there were many wolves nearby.

Chapter 4

RAILROAD NAMES

U ntil the second half of the nineteenth century, travel in Arkansas was difficult. Water was long the primary means of movement, as roads were generally primitive, and before 1860, there were only a few dozen miles of railroad. This all changed after the Civil War as railroad companies moved into and through the state, laying hundreds of miles of track and, more significantly for this book, establishing stations. The stations often became the centers for new settlements, and sometimes they attracted existing communities that had been bypassed but chose to relocate to the tracks. Railroad timetables required that stations have names. Most not built in existing towns were named for railroad personnel: executives, the surveyors and other workers, with the occasional train engineer's name for good measure. Some were named for the landowners who sold or gave the land to the railroads. Other stations were named by railroad officers for friends or benefactors and, notably, for Dutch financiers whose names were often so anglicized as to become nearly unrecognizable.

Alicia *uh-LISH-uh* (Lawrence): A railroad stop was established in 1873 and allegedly named by a railroad contractor for his wife, Alicia Swift.

Alpena: Interestingly, this town's name is of culinary origin. Straddling the Boone and Carroll county lines, this was originally a camp for workers on the Missouri and North Arkansas Railroad and called Estes. As businesses moved in, the name Alpena Pass was codified and later shortened to Alpena, allegedly the name of one of the railroad cooks.

Altheimer *ALL-timer* (Jefferson): Named for brothers Louis and Joseph Altheimer, who had invested in the area and encouraged the building of the railroad connecting Pine Bluff and Stuttgart.

Altus *ALE-tuhs* (Franklin): *Altus* is Latin for "high," and this being the highest point on (or at least close to) the railroad, it was so named by some classicist with the Little Rock and Fort Smith Railroad.

Arkinda (Little River): A trading post that served the Indian Territory across the Oklahoma border and was called Choctaw City until 1899. Then the Arkansas & Choctaw Railroad renamed it Arkinda, the latter part of the name perhaps taken from "Indian."

Atkins (Pope): There are two stories behind the name of the Pickle Capital of Arkansas. One says that when funds for extending the Little Rock & Fort Smith Railroad ran out in 1872, Massachusetts businessman Elisha Atkins raised more money, and the next crossroads was named for him. A variant says that Atkins was part of the construction team who traveled back to Boston and returned with enough funding to continue the railroad.

Aubrey (Lee): A refueling stop on the Missouri & North Arkansas Railroad. The town was created in 1907 and named for the son of a local physician, Dr. W.B. Snipes.

Banks (Bradley): A settlement built at the intersection of two railroads was originally called Morgan, but in 1906, the name was changed to honor A.B. Banks of Fordyce, who handled land purchases for the Rock Island Railroad.

Bearden (Ouachita): Named around 1882 for John T. Bearden, who was either the county judge or a lawyer for an agency of the railway's land office and helped draw up the town limits.

Beebe *BEE-bee* (White): Originally a station at the intersection of the Des Arc Road (now Highway 31) and the Cairo and Fulton Railroad and named for Roswell Beebe, who had served as president of the railroad.

Biscoe (Prairie): The Memphis and Little Rock Railroad constructed a depot on Surrounded Hill in 1871, and the post office there was originally named Fredonia. The name changed to Surrounded Hill in 1875, back to

Fredonia in 1881, then back to Surrounded Hill the same year. In 1902, the name finally became Biscoe—which it has remained, apparently because of fatigue and in order to honor landowner John Biscoe.

Blue Mountain (Logan): Settled in the late nineteenth century and originally called Maggie. The Choctaw, Oklahoma & Gulf Railroad established a depot there in 1900 and named it for a local spur of Magazine Mountain.

Boswell (Izard): Settled in the nineteenth century as a steamboat landing and originally named Wideman for the creek that ran through the town. A railroad station was built around 1905 and named for the first station agent, Robert Boswell, but the post office was named Cook, so there were simultaneously three names for the community. In 1915, the post office name was changed to Boswell as well.

Bradford (White): Settled in the nineteenth century on the White River as Grand Glaise. When the Cairo & Fulton Railroad established a depot in 1872 just to the southwest, the residents and merchants moved thither from what became Old Grand Glaise. The relocated town was first called Bradford Allen Station, perhaps for a son of Cairo & Fulton president Thomas B. Allen or, as Dean posits, for an early family named Bradford.

Brinkley (Monroe): Platted in 1869–70 on the Memphis & Little Rock Railroad at a campsite used by railroad workers, which was nicknamed Lick Skillet. The town took the more formal name for Robert Campbell Brinkley of Memphis, president of the railroad, although Deane gives Hugh Brinkley as "one of the builders" of the railroad.

Brookland (Craighead): In the 1880s, two railroads both went through the property of farmer Albert Brooks. He negotiated rights to depots and platted a town, briefly and curiously called Powell, which was quickly renamed Brookvale and then Brookland and incorporated in 1911.

Buckner (Lafayette): The town grew up around a railroad depot, originally called Barker. Its name was changed by land agent C.F. Stephens to honor Buckner Fisher, the son of a St. Louis friend.

Butterfield (Hot Spring): Established in the 1850s as a stop on the Concord Stagecoach line. It was called Womble or Wombles for the first postmaster,

Alexander Womble, but changed to Butterfield around 1892. There are three theories about this name: (1) from the famous Butterfield Stage Line, (2) a Colonel Butterfield used to visit frequently and (3) from railroad supervisor D.A. Butterfield, which would seem to be the most reasonable explanation, given that the Butterfield Line was long gone and naming towns after visitors is pretty unusual.

Cabot (Lonoke): Originally a water and fuel stop on the Cairo & Fulton Railroad, the town was apparently named after railroad executive George Cabot Ward.

Campbell Station (Jackson): Established as a depot on the Cairo and Fulton Railroad, possibly named for a railroad worker.

Carryville (Clay): Named by a railroad surveyor for his wife.

Chester (Crawford): The St. Louis–San Francisco Railway laid a line down to the town, where it built a roundhouse. The town was so named, says the story, by a railroad engineer known as Mr. Hepburn for his hometown in an unknown state.

Colt (St. Francis): A loose settlement named Taylor's Creek formed in the mid-nineteenth century along the Military Road but only developed into a town when the Helena Branch of the Iron Mountain and Southern Railroad came through and set up a depot. The local story is that a coin toss decided the name in favor of a railroad contractor named Colt, rather than store owner Nathaniel Williams's suggestion: Williamsville.

Corning: One of the two seats of Clay County. The original town, Hecht City, was named for brothers who operated a lumber mill. The town moved in 1872 to the railroad and changed its name in honor of H.D. or H.K. Corning, who was either an engineer for the construction firm that built the railroad or an official with the St. Louis, Iron Mountain and Southern Railroad and/or a wealthy pal of Jay Gould. One story says that the city leaders picked the name, hoping that Gould might look kindly on them for honoring his friend. Alas, after his initial visit, Corning never returned.

Cotter (Baxter): Established in 1902 as a station on the White River Railway near what had earlier been called Lake's Ferry. One story says it was named for a local farm family, but there is more evidence that it was named for William Cotter, a railroad manager.

Curtis (Clark): Originally a fuel depot on the Iron Mountain Railroad. The happy story is that when the first train pulled up, it was met by a lively crowd of locals. On someone's mentioning that the depot had no name, the train's engineer noted that there was no town with his name. Thus it was so christened in 1874.

Cushman (Independence): Established in 1886 when an accidental explosion killed a worker and abruptly ended construction of a trunk line into the area, where much manganese mining was going on. Originally, if unimaginatively, called Minersville, its name was changed in 1906 to honor a vice president of the St. Louis, Iron Mountain and Southern Railroad.

De Queen *DEE-kween*: The seat of Sevier County is not named for royalty. The name is an anglicization of the name of Dutch railroad financier Jan de Goeijen, whose money allowed the Kansas City Southern Railroad to get through the town of Hurrah City in 1897. De Goeijen himself, it is said, did not appreciate the well-intentioned spelling.

Donaldson (Hot Spring): A town grew up around a railroad station in the 1870s, with three stories for the name: (1) It was named for a Donaldson who owned a local sawmill; (2) The son of a railroad executive, named Donald, operated a store for residents, who referred to him as Donald's son; (3) The station and the town were named for the son-in-law of the president of the Cairo & Fulton Railroad president, which seems the most likely of the three.

Emmet (Nevada and Hempstead Counties): Developed around a station on the Cairo and Fulton Railroad, the early settlement was called Burkville. This was changed in 1874 to honor Emmet Elgin, the railroad's stationmaster.

Everton *EV-uhr-tuhn* (Boone): Established in 1901 as a depot on the Missouri and North Arkansas Railroad and perhaps named for a railroad executive or worker.

Fargo (Monroe): A settlement at the junction of the Cotton Belt and the Missouri & North Arkansas Railroads. The post office was established in

1898, and local history says that the town's name was suggested by a railroad conductor who, apparently, wished he was in North Dakota.

Fisher (Poinsett): A fuel depot on the Cotton Belt railway was built in 1883 and named for station paymaster Bud Fisher. The developing settlement was first called Fisherville, but that was quickly shortened.

Fordyce *FORE-dice*: The Dallas County seat, named for railroad executive Samuel W. Fordyce.

Garner (White): This was originally a wood depot on the Cairo & Fulton Railroad, and Joseph Garner owned the concession. The town's post office was established in 1889 and had a flurry of names, including Paxson, Clifton, Garner Station and New Garner, until 1891, when the final form became official.

Gentry (Benton): Established in 1894 along the Kansas City Southern Railroad and named for the railroad president. From 1897 until 1900, the town was called Orchard on account of the many apple producers.

Gilbert (Searcy): The Missouri & North Arkansas Railroad missed the small community of Duff by about half a mile. The residents thereupon moved en masse to Camp Gilbert, a station named for Charles W. Gilbert, the railroad president, and established a new town with his name.

Gillett (Arkansas): The town was settled in the 1880s and called Leslie Center in honor of early settlers. But the 1890 request to the USPS to use this name was denied, so the townsfolk went with Gillett for Francis M. Gillett, a financier who helped bring the railroad to town in 1895 and who became president of the Stuttgart & Arkansas Railroad.

Gillham (Sevier): There was great excitement in the nineteenth century with the reported discovery of silver in southwest Arkansas, and the town that sprouted up near the mine was naturally called Silver City. Alas, the "silver" turned out to be antimony, which resulted in less excitement and mines dedicated to that ore. When the railroad bypassed their town by a mile, the residents moved it to the tracks and gave it the name of Gillham in honor of the railroad's chief engineer, Robert Gillham.

Gould *GOOLD* (Lincoln): A depot on the Little Rock, Pine Bluff and New Orleans Railroad, first called Palmer Switch and then Joslyn. When the town was platted in 1907, the name was changed to Gould, but not necessarily for the railroad magnate. Deane speculates that it was named for Gould's daughter, Helen, who came to Star City to celebrate the extension of the Southwestern Railroad into that town in 1907.

Grannis (Polk): A railroad depot near the town of Leon Station, it was named Grannis in honor of an official of the Kansas City, Pittsburg and Gulf Railroad.

Greenway (Clay): When the town was established in the 1870s, the postmaster named it Clayville since it was in Clay County, but most residents preferred Hamburg. The railroad came through and established a station named Greenway—according to the story, for a railroad physician living in Hot Springs—and that name stuck.

Greeson, Lake (Pike): Formed in 1950 by the Narrows Dam on the Little Missouri River, which had long been advocated for by Martin White Greeson, owner of the Murfreesboro–Nashville Southwest Railroad.

Griffithville (White): A settlement was established in the 1850s but not named until 1898, when the Rock Island Railroad built a short line and named the station for the surveyor, Griffith.

Guion *GEYE-uhn* (Izard): Originally known as Wild Haw Landing when it was settled in the nineteenth century, then as Louis. Prosperity came with the St. Louis, Iron Mountain and Southern Railroad, but at the cost of the station and then the town being named to honor railroad official J.H. Guion.

Gurdon (Clark): Developed in the 1870s along the Cairo & Fulton Railroad and probably named for Gurdon Cunningham, who had surveyed the right-of-way for the railroad.

Hardy (Sharp): Developed in 1883 as a depot on the Kansas City, Springfield & Memphis Railroad. Residents wanted to name it Forty Islands after a nearby creek, but the postal service was delivering mail to the station named for a railroad contractor from Batesville, James A. Hardy, and insisted on that name.

Hartman (Johnson): In the 1880s, a railroad conductor, T. Hartman, promised to have a depot and side-track built at the settlement named Coalburg if the residents would name it for him. They did, and he did.

Hatfield (Polk): Established in the 1840s as Clayton Spur. In 1897, many residents removed a short distance to a new railroad and named their new town Morley, but that was quickly changed to Hatfield to honor a railroad worker killed in an explosion.

Hempwallace (Garland): The town of Wiggs was established in 1886, and its name was changed in 1914 to honor Hemp Wallace, a stockholder in the railroad running from Nashville to Hot Springs. Eventually, the two names were combined into one word.

Higginson (White): A depot on the Cairo & Fulton Railroad was built in 1872 and named for a railroad shareholder.

Hiwassee *hi-WAHS-see* (Benton): A railroad depot was named by an engineer for his alma mater, Hiwassee College in Tennessee. The name derives from a Cherokee word meaning "meadow," and Deane speculates that the area was so named by Cherokees on their migration.

Hope: The seat of Hempstead County and birthplace of U.S. president Bill Clinton formed around a station on the Cairo & Fulton Railroad. When it was built in 1872, the railroad bypassed Washington, which had been the county seat and quickly declined. Named for Hope Loughborough, the daughter of James Loughborough, an executive of the railroad.

Hoxie *HAHK-see* (Lawrence): Formed around 1880 when the Kansas City, Springfield and Memphis Railroad could not get land in Walnut Ridge but was offered free land by Mary A. Boas a few miles away. Named for H.M. Hoxie, an executive of the St. Louis, Iron Mountain and Southern Railroad, who helped guide the railroad in this direction.

Humphrey *UMM-free* (Arkansas and Jefferson Counties): A railroad depot established in the 1880s and named for the railway surveyor.

Jacksonville (Pulaski): Land along a proposed railroad line was bought up around 1870 by Nicholas Jackson, and the station on the land he had ceded to the Cairo & Fulton Railroad was first known as Jackson Springs and then, as of 1872, Jacksonville.

Junction City (Union): A town that grew up around the station built by the Arkansas Southern Railway Company when its track from El Dorado reached the Louisiana border. The town was originally called Junction, but the 1897 post office application asked for and received the longer name. The modern city straddles not only two states but also one county in Arkansas and two parishes in Louisiana.

Kelso (Desha): A railroad depot named for George Kelso, a surveying engineer.

Kensett *KIN-suht* (White): Thomas Kensett, of the Cairo & Fulton Railroad board of directors, was the source for the name of this 1872 railroad depot. But a local story quickly sprang up, as related by Deane: an Irish railroad construction boss, having been asked by the crew where to locate the station, wonderfully said, "You kin set it here or you kin set it here." A town in Iowa also is named for Thomas Kensett, with no tales of Irish straw bosses in sight.

Kingsland (Cleveland): A community formed in the 1880s along the Texas & St. Louis Southwestern Railroad, originally called Cohassett for a locally known Indian chief who hunted the area. The first application for a post office name, Arkatha, was denied, as was the second, Cohassett. The third suggestion, Kingsland, probably to honor a railroad official, was accepted in 1883.

Knobel *NOH-buhl* (Clay): A town that grew up near a railroad junction in the 1870s, Knobel is not to be confused with Knob, five miles east. Missouri Pacific Railroad engineer Gus Knobel is probably the source of the name.

LaCrosse (Izard): Originally called Wild Haws when it was settled in the mid-nineteenth century on account of all the haws trees. The name was changed to LaCrosse in 1869 because two railroads had surveyed the site and the town expected to become a booming crossroads. It is now abandoned.

Kingsland. *Courtesy of Greg Banic.*

Ladelle (Drew): A station was planned in 1912 where the Ashley, Drew & Northern Railroad crossed the Collins-Lacey road, and early promoter Joe Lee Allen named it for his daughter.

Lavaca *luh-VAK-uh* (Sebastian): The town of Military Grove, so named for a stand of oak trees, grew up east of Fort Smith in the 1870s and later was called Oak Bower. A railroad depot one mile to the west attracted more building, so that Oak Bower was eventually subsumed into the town allegedly called by Spanish railroad workers "the Cow." Deane speculates that this might refer to a bison cow.

Letona (White): In 1900, postmaster Asa Cox secured the name Cox for the town's post office. The local railroad depot was named Letona, either for a railroad executive or for the Roman deity Latona, and that became the town's name on its 1911 incorporation.

Louann (Ouachita): Settled after the Civil War, and local history says that the town was first called Wells, after one of the early settlers. As the railroad was being built, little Louann Wells, daughter of Albert and Mary Ann Wells, used to bring buckets of water out to the thirsty railroad workers, many of whom were boarding at the Wells farm. The grateful men got the railroad to name the station—and then the 1891 post office—in her honor. Prosperity came with the discovery of oil nearby in the 1920s.

McDougal (Clay): A railroad worker, otherwise unknown, gave his name to the 1907 depot along the track from Poplar Grove, Missouri, to Piggot, Arkansas.

Mena *MEE-nuh*: The seat of Polk County was named by the town founder, Arthur Stilwell, for the wife of Jan A. DeGoeijen, Stilwell's Dutch partner. Her name was Folmina Margaretha Janssen-de Goeijen, but thankfully, her nickname was Mena. Deane mistakenly says that Mena was de Goeijen's mother, but he does correct the widely believed story that the name was a short form of Wilhelmina—who has her own Arkansas place name.

Nettleton (Craighead): Originally a station of the Kansas City, Fort Scott & Memphis Railroad and named for George Nettleton, an official of the railroad.

Nimmons (Clay): Established around 1900 where two small railroad branches met and named either for a railroad worker or for an officer of the Campbell & Malden Lumber Company.

Paragould *PAIR-uh-goold*: The seat of Greene County was named for two railroad magnates. The town grew up at the intersection of the Texas & St. Louis Railway (later the Cotton Belt), owned by J.W. Paramore, and the St. Louis, Iron Mountain and Southern Railroad, owned by Jay Gould. The 1881 Cotton Belt station was called Parmley, and Gould's line came through in 1882. The first postmaster chose the town's name, combining the surnames of the two railroaders. Gould objected to being in second place and demanded the schedule list the town as Parmley. Deane tells a more amicable, and therefore implausible, story of compromise.

Parkdale (Ashley): A boat landing on the Bayou Bartholomew in the 1850s was named Poplar Bluffs, because of a local grove. A railroad station was built in the early 1890s, and to avoid confusion with the station of Poplar Bluffs, Missouri, the railroad called it Parkdale, and the developing town followed suit.

Parkin (Cross): Established as a depot on the St. Louis, Iron Mountain and Southern Railroad and named for William Parkin, who supervised the laying of tracks in this area.

Pettigrew (Madison): George Pettigrew, a civil engineer with the St. Louis–San Francisco Railway, laid out this town in 1897 when the railroad came through.

Poyen *POI-in* (Grant): Settled in the early nineteenth century and known, like many towns, as Cross Roads. When the Rock Island Railroad came through, the railroad president mapped out a town and named it for a French ancestor who had fled the Revolution and settled in Maine.

Poyen. *Author's collection.*

Pyatt *PEYE-uht* (Marion): Founded after the Civil War and first called Stringtown because, according to one explanation, it was strung up and down Crooked Creek. Around 1870, the town's name was changed to Powell, in honor of the Republican governor. When the Missouri Pacific Railroad bypassed Powell, town residents moved to the tracks and named their new settlement for an engineer on the railroad, or perhaps the section foreman.

Queen Wilhelmina State Park: After Arthur Stilwell, with support from Dutch investors led by Jan de Goeijen (*see* De Queen), had completed his Kansas City, Pittsburg and Gulf Railroad, he sought to create places that would draw tourists. On Rich Mountain, he built a thirty-five-room hotel, which he and de Goeijen christened the Queen Wilhelmina Inn and which included a room for the queen, should she ever visit (she never did). In the 1950s, the state legislature purchased the inn and acquired the land around it as a state park.

Ratcliff (Logan): A settlement around five natural springs grew up in the 1870s and was called National Springs, or National for short. When the Arkansas Central Railroad built a depot named for Samuel Ratcliff, a railroad engineer, a short distance away, most of the residents from National moved to the station.

Redfield (Jefferson): Platted in 1880 as a town along the Little Rock, Mississippi River and Texas Railroad and named for railroad president John E. Redfield.

Rison *REYE-zuhn*: The Cleveland County seat was founded at the end of the nineteenth century and named for William Richard Rison from Alabama, a friend and business partner of the town's founder, Samuel Wesley Fordyce. Interestingly, while Fordyce had been a Union soldier, Rison had worn Confederate gray.

Rogers (Benton): Originally the site of a tavern near a spring on Butterfield's Overland Mail Company route in the 1850s. In 1881, the St. Louis–San Francisco Railway built a station there named for Captain Charles Warrington Rogers, general manager of the Frisco.

Rohwer *ROH-uhr* (Desha): A small community that grew up next to the railroad and was first called Harding. But since Arkansas had another city named Harding, a railroad construction superintendent by the name of Rohwer offered the use of his name, which was accepted in 1913. Deane says that Rohwer was the locomotive engineer of the first train to come here.

Russell (White): Founded in the 1870s on the St. Louis and Iron Mountain Railroad as a depot and named either by employee Russell Kaufman or, as Deane thinks, for an Irish construction worker, W.T. Russell, beloved for his sense of humor. The name was changed in 1878 to Plants but back to Russell in 1878.

Shirley (Van Buren): Formed around 1909 around a depot of the Missouri & North Arkansas Railroad, near a bridge over the Little Red River, and named, almost jokingly, for the popular stationmaster named Shirley. The nearby wonderfully named town of Settlement had been bypassed, so most residents moved to Shirley, unsettling Settlement.

Stephens (Ouachita): The station built in the 1890s on the Texas & St. Louis Railway was named by a Mr. Stephens, the surveyor for the railroad. The railroad went between the towns of Richland and Seminary, both of which withered away as their residents uprooted themselves to the station in the middle. Legend says that the town, the boyhood home of historian Dee Brown, was supposed to be called Waldo, but a mapmaker got confused and gave that name to a town fifteen miles south, modern-day Waldo.

Stonewall (Greene): Joseph Collins's 1884 application to name the town, which had grown up around a depot on the Iron Mountain Railroad, Collinsville was rejected. Because the railway had built up some levees with stones along the river, the town's nickname had been Stonewall, so this, and not the Confederate general, was the basis of the second—and successful—submission to the post office.

Strong (Union): A railroad depot on the El Dorado and Bastrop Railroad was christened Victoria by surveyor William Strong, and so the settlement was incorporated. But local landowner James Solomon Coleman had been calling the depot Strong in honor of the surveyor. When the post office was going to open in 1904, the existence of another Victoria in Arkansas led to the official name change. But as late as the 1940s, many locals still called the town Victoria. The station attracted the residents of nearby Concord, a mile south, which despite the official name had long been called Bucksnort, ostensibly but implausibly because of young men on a bender and "snorting around."

Traskwood (Saline): The 1870s railroad depot was allegedly named for two rail workers, Trask and Wood.

Trumann (Poinsett): In 1896, the company town of Mosher was established by the lumber company of that name. But in 1902, the Weona Land Company insisted that the name be changed to Weona, with partisans for both names holding fast. Since neither company would accept the name of the other, they compromised, and the town's name was changed in 1904 to Trumann, honoring a New York railroad executive named Truman. The post office threw in the extra *n* for good measure.

Vandervoort *VAN-duhr-vuhrt* (Polk): A stop on the Kansas City, Pittsburg & Gulf Railroad, it was originally called Janssen, the maiden name of railroad financier Jan de Goeijen's wife. But because another town was already named Jansen, in 1907, the town was renamed Vandervoort, the maiden name of de Goeijen's mother. *See also* Mena.

Waldo (Columbia): A depot on the St. Louis, Arkansas and Texas Railroad, named in 1884 for a freight agent, was established three miles south of the town of Lamartine, which pretty much moved to the new location. The postmaster tried to get it called New Lamartine, but the railroad had other ideas and insisted on Waldo. (*But see* Stephens.)

Weiner *WEE-nuhr* (Poinsett): Originally called West Prairie when it was settled in 1870. When the St. Louis & Southwest Railroad came through and built a depot, it was named in honor of a St. Louis railroad official. Allsopp says that the official's name was Wiener but the USPS misspelled it.

Welcome (Columbia): Just across the state line from Springhill, Louisiana. The railroad depot built in the 1890s was named Welcome Depot, and so the community took on the friendly name.

Wickes (Polk): Established in 1897 along the Kansas City, Pittsburg & Gulf Railroad, the town was first called Sherwood, but that was quickly changed to honor Thomas Wickes, a vice president of the Pullman Company. Deane repeats a bogus tale that the town was first called

Winfield, for a family, and renamed because of a vendor coming through the town hawking candlewicks.

Wilmot (Ashley): Established as a steamboat stop on the Bayou Bartholomew in the middle of the nineteenth century, the early community resolutely called itself Enterprise. The 1880 post office was called Bartholomew, but the town name became Wilmot around 1892, allegedly for a railroad surveyor.

Wilton (Little River): When Richmond residents refused the Texarkana & Northern Railroad permission to build through their town, Paschal S. Kinsworthy and Sergent Prentiss Mills offered their land, and so the settlement was named Millkin in 1891 in honor of both founders. But in 1892, the railroad highhandedly changed the depot name to Wilton because one of the principal stockholders was from Wilton, England.

Winslow (Washington): Originally a mountaintop station on the Woolum-Brown Stage Line, established in 1876 and known as Summit Home. With the coming in 1881 of the St. Louis–San Francisco Railroad, the town was renamed for Edward F. Winslow, president of the railroad.

Witherspoon (Hot Spring): The town that grew up around an 1873 railroad station on the Cairo & Fulton Railroad was named for James Witherspoon of Arkadelphia, an early director of that line.

Chapter 5

POST OFFICE NAMES

When a community grew large enough, the postal service would establish an office in a central location, usually a general store, triggering the need for a name by which to identify the place. Since it was the town's postmaster (often as not, the owner of the store) who sent in to Washington the official application for a name, that person wielded significant influence over what name was submitted. Many postmasters used their own name or, if not their last name, perhaps the name of their spouse or even child.

When the handwritten application was received in Washington, interesting things might happen. Generally, the Post Office approved the application, but in many cases, because there was already a post office with that name, the application was denied and the town required to submit another name. And every so often, bemused officials had trouble deciphering the handwritten application, with interesting results. Although it was officially the Post Office of the United States, it is called the USPS in this book to avoid confusion with local post offices.

Agnos *AG-nuhs* (Fulton): The town was first called Crossroads, but the USPS rejected that proposed name in the 1880 application for a post office. The story goes that the blacksmith, at whose shop the mail was delivered, couldn't think of another name, so he chose the name of his wife, Agnes. Some USPS clerk thereupon garbled it. Deane says that Agnes was the daughter of a local family.

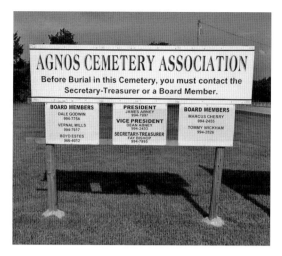

Agnos. *Courtesy of Tom Cendoanni.*

Apt (Craighead): A small unnamed settlement until the railroad came through in 1882, which required that the residents tell the USPS the name of their town. As the residents debated, one is supposed to have said, "Oh, well, I suppose they [the post office] will be apt to name the place," and the group seized on that for the name.

Arbaugh (Newton): The post office was established in 1928, with the first postmistress being Mrs. Rebecca Arbaugh, daughter-in-law of the first settler, Albert Arbaugh, who settled in 1868: Arbaughs wherever you look!

Banner (Cleburne): Settled in the mid-nineteenth century and first called Round Pond. There was a Bonner family in the area, and two Bonners were postmasters at nearby Alonzo, so the best guess is that this is another misspelling by the USPS.

Barney (Faulkner): Probably named for Barney Heffington, store owner and postmaster.

Batavia (Boone): The first postmaster, R.E. Underwood, came from and named his post office for Batavia, New York.

Battles (Izard): Established in the late nineteenth century and originally named Hamm for settler A.J. Hamm. The post office was closed briefly around 1910, then reopened and named for postmaster F.M. Battle, but why the name was made plural is not known.

Bergman (Boone): Settled in the late nineteenth century and at first called Clabby, the town was finally named for postmistress Edith Bergman.

Blackwell (Conway): Established after 1872 around a station on the Little Rock & Fort Smith Railroad and first called Blackville, for no recorded reason. After a contentious debate on a name for the 1878 post office, the residents settled on Blackwell. One story says that the town was named for William Black, the first postmaster, who was a Black man.

Bono (Craighead): Established in 1883 by area farmer Alfred Bonner, but the U.S. Post Office denied the name Bonnerville in order to avoid confusion with the town of Booneville. Town residents thereupon held a contest and picked the name Bono.

Bono (Faulkner): Settled in the late nineteenth century and first called Kendall, for the first postmaster. The town later changed its name to honor early settler William Bono, who had changed his name from the French Bonneau.

Botkinburg (Van Buren): Named by postmaster Purne Botkin, whose first name would also have made for an interesting town name.

Buford (Baxter): The town was named by postmaster George Osborn in honor of his son.

Caldwell (St. Francis): Originally a depot on the St. Louis, Iron Mountain and Southern Railroad, it was named for postmaster Thomas B. Caldwell, who perhaps was the son of early settler William Caldwell.

Canfield (Lafayette): Platted in 1877, and the 1888 post office was named for Eugene H. Canfield, the first postmaster.

Caulksville *CORKS-vul* (Logan): Robert Caulk is said to have arrived in the area in the 1830s and received a land patent in 1860. He opened a post office in 1870 in the town named for his family.

Center Ridge (Conway): Founded in 1878 and, apparently, named for a decrepit post office about five miles north on a ridge that was a watershed for two creeks.

Cherry (Clark): The post office, which existed from 1906 to 1910, was named by the postmistress, Lizzie Cherry.

Chimes (Van Buren): When the USPS needed a name for a post office to serve a number of small communities, they asked postmaster Jesse N. O'Neal for a short and unique name. He based his suggestion on the title of a new song book, *Chimes*, and the name was approved in 1914.

Clarkedale (Crittenden): Settled early in the nineteenth century and called Greenock, the town was the county seat until 1836. After the Civil War, the St. Louis–San Francisco Railroad came through, and Cleaveland (or Cleveland) Clarke opened a store, became postmaster and changed the town name to Clarkton. The name was changed in 1910 to Clarkedale but is sometimes spelled Clarkdale.

Clarkridge (Baxter): Settled before 1820, the town was not incorporated for a century. The 1924 post office was in the home of postal carrier and unorthodox shoemaker George J. Clark, nicknamed "Wooden Bottom" because he made shoes with wooden soles.

Convenience (Independence): This hamlet that existed in the second half of the nineteenth century provides a good story: the postmaster, unable to think of a name for the town, simply asked the U.S. Post Office to pick a name "at your convenience."

Cowell (Newton): Established in 1902 and named for Joab A. Cowell, an early settler and singing teacher and the town's first postmaster.

Diaz *DYE-az* (Jackson): Founded in the mid-nineteenth century and called Shiloh. When the railroad came through, a station was built, named for Jackson County resident Joseph Dyas, a conductor, and the postal service seems to have misread the application.

Erbie (Newton): According to the story, the town was established in 1915 and the name selected by the USPS from a handful of suggestions gathered by the residents.

Evansville (Washington): Postmaster Lewis Evans chose the name when the post office was established in 1838.

Fannie (Montgomery): After having had two non-starter names, Liberty and Red Haw, the town was named for its first postmistress, Mrs. Fannie Wilson.

Guy (Faulkner): Although a settlement was established in 1842, it wasn't until 1890 that the town had a post office, which was named by the postmaster for his grandson. There is no record of what the settlement's name had been for its first fifty years.

Hattieville (Conway): Postmaster William W. Stout was born at nearby Stout's Chapel. Judging that there were enough Stouts when applying for a post office in 1884, he chose the name of his wife, Hattie Peck Stout.

Higden (Cleburne): Settled in the late nineteenth century and first called Salt Springs Barrens. The first post office in 1894 was called Channel for a feature in the Little Red River, but in 1895, the name was changed to honor early resident Thomas G. Higdon, although the USPS misread the application.

Hopper (Montgomery): When it was settled in the early nineteenth century, the town was called Parks after the donor of land for a school, Jack Parks. After the Civil War, William J. Hopper opened a store where people dropped off mail, so the post office was named for his store.

Hugh (Carroll): Originally and astonishingly called Hottentot when it was founded in 1890. A decade later, the name was changed to Hough or Hugh in 1899, perhaps because of postmistress Maggie Hughes.

Hunt (Johnson): M.H. Hunt settled this town after the Civil War and asked for the name Stonewall. The USPS rejected that and assigned the name Huntsville, later dropping the "ville." Also known locally as Hunt Town.

Ida (Cleburne): Established after the Civil War, and the first postmaster named the town after his sister.

Jumbo (Izard): In another botched effort by the USPS, this town was, according to the story, named for leading citizen "Jimbo" Smith, whose nickname was garbled by the Post Office, and the town became forevermore Jumbo.

Lafe (Green): German immigrants in the 1880s established a town around a railroad depot that was originally called Newberry. The post office refused this name, so the postmaster crafted the name Loulyma from the first names of his three daughters—Louise, Lily and Mary. Townsfolk stubbornly held onto Newberry, but finally, in 1901, all parties agreed on the nickname of a prominent merchant and postmaster, Lafeyette Mueller.

McHue (Independence): Settled in the early nineteenth century in the Ed Taylor Holler and initially called Gilbert Spring. In the later part of the century, the name was changed to one combining the names of the postmaster and his wife, William Mayhue and Cynthia McClendon Mayhue.

Nail (Newton): Deane relates a locally popular folk story: a bunch of men are sitting around and arguing about possible names, and one guy picks up a rusty nail and says to name the town after it. Almost certainly true, if not nearly as colorful, is that the town was established before 1914 and named for the second postmaster, George W. Neal, with the usual USPS mangling of the name.

Noland (Randolph): Nova Pyland was the first postmistress, and a W.H. Skinner attained local fame by coining the town's name from parts of hers.

Norphlet *NOR-flight* (Union): A railroad depot was reportedly named for Nauphlet Goodwin, but the name was garbled by the USPS when the post office was established in 1891.

Ola (Yell): Settled in the mid-nineteenth century with the marvelous name of Red Lick, the town changed its name in 1866 to Petit Jean, after the river on which it was then located. In 1880, when the town was seeking a post office, the USPS balked at Petit Jean and demanded another name. At that, the residents sought to rename the town for prominent citizen J.M. Harkey, whose mill was the center of the settlement. Harkey suggested the name of his daughter, Ola, which the residents and the USPS all approved. Deane's tale of the USPS asking Harkey for a suggestion makes no sense, unless it was the local postmaster who made the request. In any case, the Petit Jean River has changed course, and now only an oxbow lake remains.

Onia *OH-nee* or *ah-NEE-uh* (Stone): Settled in the mid-nineteenth century and called Lower Clark. When a post office was sought in 1908, the postmaster suggested naming it after the winner of an upcoming beauty contest. The winner was Malinda Iona Balentine, whose nickname was Ona or Onie, but the postal service bureaucrat thought that Onie was a misspelling and changed it to Onia. Since Balentine or Iona or even Malinda would seem to have been more obvious names for a town, the likelihood of this tale being true seems slim.

Parks (Scott): An agricultural community settled in the 1830s and first named White Church for the Methodist church building. In 1838, it was renamed for the county judge and first postmaster, Cyrus Parks.

Peel (Marion): Imaginatively called Need More when it was settled in the early nineteenth century, after the Civil War, the post office was established and named for postmaster Sam Peel.

Pelsor (Pope): In her 1922 application for a post office, postmistress Loretta Pelsor requested the name by which the town had always been known, Sand Gap. Perhaps confused, the USPS assigned the town the name of Pelsor instead, and that remains the official name. Undaunted, residents still call their town Sand Gap.

Prattsville (Grant): Settled in the 1840s and named for John Pratt, the first postmaster and owner of a local ferry across the Saline River.

Prim (Cleburne): Settled in the nineteenth century and first called California, in 1892 it was named by the first postmaster, George Washington Prim.

Revilee (Logan): In 1830, Charles Humphry built his home, which he named Reveille, and the town that grew up around it served briefly as the seat of Sarber County. In 1848, the town's application for a post office was approved and the name, not surprisingly, mangled.

Rhea *RAY* (Washington): Settled around 1830 by Pleasant V. Rhea but named for mill owner—and the town's second postmaster—William H. Rhea, explaining why the town was also called Rhea's Mills.

Rowell *ROW-uhl* (Cleveland): The town was settled in the middle of the nineteenth century and first called Centerville; its name was changed to St. John in 1868. In 1880, the name was changed to Mackville, and finally, in 1884, it was renamed for the postmaster, William S. Rowell.

Royal (Garland): When the town was established in 1906, postmaster Joel Rice submitted to the USPS the names of his two sons, Joel and Royal.

Rushing (Stone): Settled after the Civil War and named for the first postmaster, Ephraim "Eaf" Rushing.

Snowball (Searcy): There had been some mills in the area called Calf Creek, but a town developed in the 1880s around a new Masonic lodge, named Snow Hall for the local sheriff, Benjamin "Uncle Ben" Franklin Snow. The 1888 application for the post office was misread by postal officials, and thence came the town name.

Story (Montgomery): Named in 1886 for either the first postmistress, Nellie Story, or her husband, James, who built the store housing the post office.

Sturkie (Fulton): In 1894, postmaster William Sturkie, originally from South Carolina, proposed the name Bay Creek, but the USPS denied that and, without consultation, named it Sturkie.

Summers (Washington): Settled around 1880 and named for early postmaster John F. Summers.

Thida (Independence): Developed in the nineteenth century, the settlement was first known as Liberty Hill. When applying for a post office in 1922, residents acceded to the wishes of J.W. Caldwell, who had been impressed by the baby daughter of friends, named Thyda Raye Rutledge. Alas, the USPS changed the spelling to Thida.

Timbo (Stone): This town was settled in the mid-nineteenth century, and the name on the 1886 post office application was that of the postmaster's brother, James "Jimbo" Maloy. A USPS bureaucrat misread the *J* as a *T*.

Vanndale *VAN-dayl* (Cross): John Maget Vann, the local store owner and postmaster, was the source of the town's name. When the Iron Mountain Railroad bypassed the town, Vann simply built a new store by the tracks and kept the post office name at his new location.

Viola (Fulton): When the town was established around 1850, it was named by the first postmaster, Newton Barker, in honor of his hometown of Viola,

Kentucky. He also named his daughter Viola, which has led to confusion about the town being named for her.

Wayton (Newton): Established in 1892 and named for the first postmistress, Louise A. Way.

Willisville (Nevada): Settled after the Civil War and first called Tyson's Store, then changed in 1893, apparently to honor the postmaster, Willis G. Herring.

Wilmar *WIL-muhr* (Drew): The original landowner since 1859, farmer James Thomas Dionysius Anderson, built a sawmill and opened a post office in 1884, naming it in honor of his daughter Willie Elvira Anderson.

Witcherville (Sebastian): Established in the 1850s and named for William J. Witcher from Virginia, an early postmaster.

Chapter 6

RELIGIOUS AND ETHNIC NAMES

In 1673, a party of Frenchmen arrived in what would become Arkansas, led by Jesuit Jacques Marquette, and French explorers and trappers continued to travel its rivers and paths for many years. Place names with French spellings, or variations thereof, are a legacy of their presence, especially in the southern part of the state. As White settlers moved in through the thickly forested delta, their initial settlements were small. The nature of farming in the east, characterized by large plantations, and the hills and ravines of the west limited the size of towns. In the rugged Ozarks and Ouachitas, towns would grow up around the first building in a settlement, which was usually a church, and often take its name.

After the Civil War, many formerly enslaved persons remained close to where they had been in servitude, while others established new communities for themselves and for other former slaves who migrated in large numbers from other states. The railroads brought in other new settlers, especially members of ethnic groups that had been recruited by the state or the railroads. Many of these new Arkansans brought their Catholic faith, and their town names reflected their heritage. Other new arrivals added their special flavors to the ethnic and spiritual cadences of the names of Arkansas.

Ain. *Author's collection.*

Ain (Grant): The town had a post office by 1879, and one story says that it was named for a town in biblical Galilee.

Antioch (Craighead): A suburb of Brookland, named for the city so prominent in the New Testament.

Antioch (White): The post office opened in 1887, and the name was that of a local church.

Augsburg (Pope): Settled around 1883 by German Lutherans and named for the German castle so central to Martin Luther's career.

Avilla (Saline): Settled in 1881 by immigrants from Saxony who called their community Kilonie Hoffnung ("Hope Colony"), but apparently the 1881 post office was called Avilla, with no record of why.

Beryl (Faulkner): Local history says it was named by an early settler for the precious stone mentioned in the Bible.

Bethel Heights (Benton): Settled around the time of the Civil War and called both Bethel and Newkirk, for the family that had donated land for the school. There is no record of how the "Heights" got added.

Avilla. *Author's collection.*

Bethesda *buh-THEZ-duh* (Independence): Established as Washington in the late nineteenth century and named in reference to the biblical healing pool in Jerusalem.

Canaan (Searcy): Named for the biblical region. Also called Horton Bend. By the mid-nineteenth century, there was a Canaan Cemetery.

Catholic Point (Conway): Established after 1878 as a community for Italian immigrants and named for their faith.

Center Hill (Greene): As a town grew up in the middle of the nineteenth century around the Center Hill Baptist Church, it took the church's name. This church had first been called Cedar Hill, and the official story is that the name was changed to note how the church was in the center of several hills. Whether that is true or there was confusion between "center" and "cedar" is left to the imagination.

Concord (Cleburne): In 1877, the church of the postwar settlement needed a name, and the congregation hopefully chose Concord. The name eventually was used for the settlement and became official when the post office was established in 1905.

Culpepper Mountain (Van Buren): The Reverend C.H. Culpepper was the first pastor of the settlement's Methodist Episcopal Church South but moved away after losing two sons, both buried near the church.

Curia *CUE-ree*: A creek and lake in Independence County and a town named for the creek. The name Bayou Cure is listed in an 1820 description of the county, and other spellings have included Bayou Cure and Cura Creek. There has been speculation about a priest's visit to local Catholic settlers but no rationale as to how that would rate a creek's name.

Damascus (Van Buren & Faulkner Counties): Settled in the 1870s and called Hutto, after the first resident. When they applied for a post office in 1887, the town residents went with Hutto's suggestion of the Syrian city's name.

Egypt. Courtesy of city-data.com.

Egypt (Craighead): A once prosperous farming and timber town grew up around 1900, and avid lumber promoters named the township Promised Land. But Egypt had been for many years and remained the name of the town, allegedly because its agricultural wealth resembled the legendary resources of Ancient Egypt. Deane aptly quotes a letter from the descendant of a settler, also noting nearby Canaan Creek: "Our ancestors gave some thought to Bible reading."

Goshen (Washington): Since the early nineteenth century, this has been the site of a Methodist campground, and the town was incorporated only in 1982.

Jerusalem (Conway): Deane repeats the tale of a customer at the local general store who complained that the road, which led to no place in particular, was "like going from Jericho to Jerusalem." A delightful if nonsensical story.

Little Flock (Benton): The town, incorporated only in 1976, is named for the historic Little Flock Primitive Baptist Church, which was organized in 1843 and took its name from Luke 12:32. There's another church with this name in Logan County.

Little Italy (Pulaski and Perry Counties): Founded in 1915 by Italians and called Alta Villa, then later Little Italy, which sounded more American.

Lutherville (Johnson): Established in 1882 by German Lutherans on land sold by the Missouri Pacific Railroad Company and the site of anti-German violence during World War I.

Macedonia (Cleveland): The community is named for the Macedonia Free Will Baptist Church, which was organized in 1902.

McJester (Cleburne): Local history suggests that the USPS mangled the requested name, that of a local family, the McLesters.

Mount Judea *JOO-dee* (Newton): Established in 1856 and named for the biblical region.

Mozart *MOH-zart* (Stone): This town was homesteaded after the Civil War, and the 1926 post office name was requested by Austrian immigrant farmers, in honor of their famous composer.

Nimrod, town (Perry) and lake (Yell): This wonderfully named town was settled prior to the Civil War and allegedly named by the first postmaster for the biblical hunter in Genesis 10. There is also speculation, more probable if less fun, that some early settlers came from Nimrod Hill, Tennessee.

O'Kean (Randolph): A small Catholic settlement that developed after the Civil War, it was a stop on the regular itinerary of Father James O'Kean, and so the name came about. The arrival of the railroad led to significant growth in the late nineteenth century.

Palestine *PAL-uh-steen* (St. Francis): Given its name in 1870, either for a fatally injured sawmill employee named Palestine or because the first postmaster, who happened to be Jewish, picked the name of the Holy Land.

Palmyra (Lincoln): Myra Collins, daughter of an early settler, is one possible source for the name of this town, settled in the 1870s—as is the city in Syria. The town was also called, oddly, Sixteenth, being at one time in the sixteenth section of Drew County.

Patmos (Hempstead): A refueling depot for the Louisiana and Arkansas Railway and named by the residents in 1903 for the Greek island where St. John received the Revelations.

Pisgah (Pike): The biblical mountain was the source of the name of this town, established after the Civil War.

Prague *PRAYG* (Grant): Bohemians and Slovaks came here from Chicago in the 1910s and named their town for the European city.

St. Charles (Arkansas): Charles Belknap platted a town in 1839 that was first known as Belknap's Bluff, and almost certainly the 1850 post office was named for Belknap's patron saint. Deane, oddly, surmises that it was named for Spanish king Carlos, albeit with Belknap's approval.

St. Elizabeth (Conway): Established in the 1870s by German Catholic immigrants and named for the thirteenth-century Hungarian saint.

St. Francis County: The county was named for the **St. Francis River**, which itself was probably named by the Marquette and Joliet expedition, probably for the saint from Assisi, but this is not certain. Spanish soldiers likewise called it the Rio San Francisco. The town in Clay County was originally a ferry across the St. Francis river and was named Chalk Bluff for that salient geological feature. A railroad depot constructed a couple miles downriver attracted the town's residents thither and was later renamed for the river.

St. Joe (Searcy): Settled in the middle of the nineteenth century and reportedly called Monkey Run but more decorously named Saint Joe when the post office arrived in 1877, probably because some of the town's residents had come from St. Joseph, Missouri.

St. Paul (Madison): Established in the 1830s as Scully. In 1887, the St. Louis–San Francisco Railway missed the town, so most residents relocated from what became known first as Old St. Paul, then Mills and then faded away. The new town was first called Louisa but quickly became St. Paul.

St. Vincent (Conway): Deane says that the town was first called Pigeon Roost on account of the thousands of passenger pigeons that roosted on the nearby mountain. In the 1880s, settlers along the railroad built a church with help from friends in St. Vincent, Pennsylvania, and so they gratefully took the name.

Salem (Saline): Established in the 1850s around the Salem Methodist Church.

Salem: The Fulton County seat was established in the 1840s and known as Pilot Hill. The name was changed to Salem in 1872, perhaps because by the 1850s, the Methodists had named the region the Salem Circuit.

Sardis (Saline): Established in the 1870s around the Sardis Methodist Church, which was so named by an original church member for one of the seven cities named in the Book of Revelation.

Siloam Springs *SEYE-LOHM* (Benton): When it was settled around 1840, the town was called Hico, a Cherokee word meaning "clear water." In 1880, the name was changed first to Siloam City and then to Siloam Springs as a reference to the healing waters of Jerusalem and in hopes of attracting more visitors.

Slovak (Prairie): Established in the 1890s as a settlement for Slavic immigrants and first called Slovactown.

Smyrna (Clark): Developed in the nineteenth century, the settlement was first called Clear Springs but changed its name to agree with the Smyrna Methodist Church.

Stuttgart *STUTT-gart* (Arkansas): One of the two seats of Arkansas County, it was established at Gum Pond in the mid-nineteenth century by German immigrants and named by the Lutheran minister George Adam Buerkle for the German city.

Subiaco *soo-bi-AK-oh* (Logan): The Benedictine Abbey and the nearby town, both settled around 1878, are named for the town in Italy where St. Benedict founded his first hermitage. Deane says that the early Italian immigrants were struck by the area's physical resemblance to the geography of their homeland.

Vimy Ridge Fire Department. *Author's collection.*

Ulm *ULL-im* Prairie County: Settled by German immigrants in the 1880s and first called Payer, the town was quickly renamed for the city in Bavaria whence many of the settlers had come.

Vimy Ridge (Saline): Established in 1894 as Germania, which was changed during World War I in honor of a battle won by Canadian troops in 1917. Many businesses scrubbed their German heritage from their names, but no other Arkansas town is named for Canadian battle prowess.

Watson Chapel (Jefferson): A settlement grew up around the Cumberland Presbyterian Church, which was eventually named for pastor Benjamin Watson. The town was incorporated into Pine Bluff in 1977.

White Hall (Jefferson): One story says that settlers in the late nineteenth century were drawn to clear springs, and the nearby church, called a "white hall," became a landmark. A less likely tale attributes the name to a man named Hall, who had located the springs, and an itinerant preacher named White.

Wirth (Sharp): This community developed in the second half of the nineteenth century with a number of German immigrants, including Edward B. Wirth, and the town may be named for him.

Zion (Izard): There are many churches, cemeteries and chapels with this biblical name.

Chapter 7

COMMERCIAL AND BUSINESS NAMES

Many Arkansas towns grew up around a primary business: sawmills, cotton gins and general stores often saw communities develop to provide workers and resources to support the enterprise. In many cases, these settlements were named for the owner of the town's primary business. Settlements also celebrated the products that provided the jobs, be they agricultural or mineral. Natural springs, in particular, gave their names to the towns that hoped to draw new businesses needing fresh water or visitors seeking health in the mineral baths. And sometimes, residents chose names intended to lure settlers or investors, names often more hopeful than descriptive.

Amagon *AM-uh-gun* (Jackson): Originally called Red Hill, the town was renamed for lumber businessman A.M. Ragon, dropping the first letter of his surname.

Armorel *ar-muhr-EL* (Mississippi): One of the company towns built by Robert E. Lee Wilson for his lumber workers and sharecroppers. Wilson coined the name using "Ar" for Arkansas, "Mo" for Missouri and his initials, REL.

Ashdown: The seat of Little River County was originally called Turkey Flats and then Keller. A story says that when one of his sawmills burned down in 1890, Judge Lawrence Alexander Byrne of Texarkana determined to rebuild it and to found a town called Ashdown.

Bauxite Post Office. *Author's collection.*

Back Gate (Desha): In the 1930s, the WPA built a community center across the road from the back gate of the Cross plantation.

Bauxite *BAWX-ite* (Saline): Bauxite ore was discovered here in 1887 and a mine established, which became very profitable, especially during the two world wars. The small company-run settlement nearby was first called Perrysmith for a major stockholder, Robert S. Perry, but its name was changed to Bauxite in 1903. When the Alcoa company drew down operations and ceased its civic support in 1969, the town foundered for a few years but was incorporated in 1973 and is again thriving.

Beirne *BURN* (Clark): Established in the 1870s as a lumber camp by James Lewis Beirne, who called the settlement York, but in 1880, it was officially renamed.

Bella Vista (Benton): Developed in the early twentieth century as a resort. The name was the winning entry of a contest among the residents that carried a $500 prize.

Bigelow (Perry): Cottonwood was supposed to be the original name of this town, which gave way to Esau. In 1902, the Fourche River Lumber Company set up shop as a subsidiary of the Bigelow Brothers & Walker Company of Chicago and duly changed the name.

Bonanza *buh-NAN-zuh* (Sebastian): Coal mines were opened in the area in the 1890s, and the settlement took a name more hopeful than descriptive.

Boxley (Newton): The town was established in the 1840s and first called Whiteley's Mill for the owner of a small mill. The name was later changed to honor a larger miller named William Boxley.

Burdette *bur-DETT* (Mississippi): A company town of the Three States Lumber Company of Wisconsin, incorporated in 1905 and named for Alfred Burdette Wolverton, one of the first lumbermen to settle in the area.

Calamine (Sharp): Settled in the 1840s when mills took advantage of water power, the town grew after the 1850 discovery of zinc in the area. There are two stories about the name: either it is from the mineral Calamine or for a female mine owner named Callie, who ran the "Callie mine"—which is a nicer story, because what town wants to be named for a topical medicine?

Carbon City (Logan): Established prior to the Civil War as St. Anne, a halfway point between Caulksville and Paris. Coal was discovered in 1866, and as the railroad brought real prosperity, the name was changed to reflect the town's greatest resource.

Coal Hill (Johnson): The town was named, after a couple of tries, for the coal in the area that provided jobs. Established as the terminal of a switch track, the station was originally called Whalen's Switch. In 1876, when trying to get a post office, the residents tried the name Moseville, for early settler Mose Butts, but Butts himself plumped for the eventual name.

Coaldale (Scott): Established in 1903 and named on account of the coal mines in the region.

Cotton Plant (Woodruff): Settled in the 1820s and called Richmond, probably for the Virginia city. In the 1840s, it became famous for cotton, and when Richmond was rejected as a post office name, the town leaders in 1852 opted to celebrate their agricultural wealth with the name Cotton Plant.

Crossett *KRAHS-it* (Ashley): Established around 1900 by three investors from Davenport, Iowa, including Edward Savage Crossett, who founded the Crossett Lumber Company.

Denieville (Independence): A lime-mining community in the late nineteenth century, named for the plant owner and postmaster Milton R. Denie.

Denning (Franklin): Established in the 1890s by Benjamin Denning, from the Western Coal & Mining Company, which eventually opened six mines.

Diamond (Pope): Deane tells the tale of a resident noting that the new mail route traced the shape of a diamond, which is less likely than the town founders wanting to highlight their proximity to the diamond mine near Murfreesboro.

Diamond City (Boone): Established in 1960 on the shore of the newly created Bull Shoals Lake, incorporating Sugarloaf, which had succeeded Dubuque. The name was probably generated in order to attract tourists.

Dierks (Howard): Settled in the mid-nineteenth century and first, with refreshing candor, called Hardscrabble. After the Dierks Lumber and Coal Company moved into the area and the economy boomed, the town was renamed for the four Dierks brothers who owned the multistate company.

Estico (Jackson): Early industrialist E.S. Seqwich built here a cross-tie plant, E.S. Tie Co., whence comes the name.

Evadale *EE-vuh-dayl* (Mississippi): One of the towns named by R.E. Lee Wilson, this one for his niece Eva Davies.

Evening Star (Searcy); *see* Morning Star: Deane says the town was named for the Evening Star zinc and lead mining company and that the nearby town of Morning Star's name was chosen to match this.

Fairfield Bay (Van Buren & Cleburne Counties): Formed in the 1960s on the shore of newly made Greers Ferry Lake as a retirement community. Deane says that founder Neal Simonson was on the phone in Fairfield, New Jersey, when he was told he needed a name, he took it and his company became Fairfield Communities Inc. "Bay" was added for the Arkansas community.

Farmington (Washington): Settled in the 1830s and first called Engels Mill for the local millowner. After the Civil War, Engels led the rebuilding of the town, which he named Farmington to honor the area farmers.

Felsenthal (Union): The Felsenthal Lumber Company established the town around 1900, and the town gave its name to the nearby wildlife refuge.

Gin City (Lafayette): Named not, alas, for alcohol but for the cotton ginning.

Golden City (Logan): One of the boomtowns of the Arkansas Gold Rush. It was founded in 1886 and abandoned almost at once when residents learned that the mine had been salted with gold nuggets.

Hensley (Pulaski): A railroad depot named Hensley Station on Campbell Bayou opened near the lumber mill owned first by William Campbell and then by his son-in-law, William B. Hensley. The "Station" was dropped by 1882.

Jerome (Drew): A sawmill town, first called Blissville for the Blissville Lumber Company. The company was renamed the Jerome Hardwood Lumber Company, in honor of the sawmill owner's son, Jerome Moehler, and the town took on the company's new name around 1900.

Jerome Gin. *Courtesy of the Library of Congress Prints and Photographs Division.*

Keiser (Mississippi): Another of Robert E. Lee Wilson's company towns, this was built on top of an earlier settlement called Savage Crossing to support Wilson's lumber workers and sharecroppers. Wilson changed the town's name to honor his friend John Keiser.

Kimberley (Pike): A town quickly grew up after a prospector found diamonds and was named for the South African city, perhaps in the hope of it being a similarly rich minefield. The diamond mine proved a bust, however.

King (Sevier): Established in the late 1880s, the settlement around the King-Ryder Lumber Company prospered after the Kansas City Southern Railroad built a spur there in 1897. The town was happy to call itself King's Spur, but in 1906, the post office settled for the shorter name King.

Lead Hill (Boone): Deane says that the town was first called Centerville, but since there was already a town by that name, the town had to pick another name when it incorporated. Residents named it for what were hoped to be (but were not) large deposits of lead. After World War II, the construction of the Bull Shoals Dam forced residents to move the town to higher ground. Some moved even farther and formed **South Lead Hill**.

Marie (Mississippi): One of the company towns established in the late nineteenth century by Robert E. Lee Wilson to support his sharecroppers, and named for his youngest daughter.

Monte Ne *MAHN-tuh NAY* (Benton): Established in the nineteenth century as Silver Springs. In 1900, miner and promoter William H. "Coin" Harvey bought 320 acres and concocted a name using an Italian word and an alleged Indian one meaning "mountain water." Harvey said he had asked an Indian woman for a list of words describing water, which were all too long for use except for *ne*. An indefatigable promoter, he made his retreat into a popular tourist destination, but the area is now mostly covered by Beaver Lake.

Okay *oh-KAY* (Howard): This company town was constructed in 1929 to provide housing for the workers at Ideal Cement Company's Arkansas Portland O.K. Cement Company. The location for the factory was chosen for its plentiful deposits of limestone and chalk, and the town's spectacular name was the brand name of the cement manufactured there.

Ozark Lithia (Garland): A late-nineteenth-century resort that aimed to attract customers by noting that the local waters flowing into the valley were rich in lithium.

Peach Orchard (Clay): Though there are no peach trees anymore, when Pierre Le Mieux (Americanized Peter LeMew) established a settlement that he called Petit Baril, he may have planted peach trees, because the residents were soon calling the settlement Peach Orchards. The 1892 railroad station was called Peach Tree, and by 1900, there were several orchards in the vicinity.

Perla (Hot Spring): Adalbert Strauss, president of Malvern Lumber Co., established this town to support his operations and named it for his oldest daughter, Perla Marie.

Ponca (Newton): The Ponca City (Oklahoma) Mining Company established this as a company town in 1903.

Rosboro (Pike): Lumberman Thomas "Whit" Rosborough first tried to build a sawmill near Amity, but his employment of Black workers was not tolerated there, so he moved his operation and built his own company town.

Scranton (Logan): Established around 1910 by mining investors who hoped the name would attract favorable comparison with the Pennsylvania city. It didn't.

Standard-Umsted or **Umpstead** (Ouachita): A company town established in the 1920s for workers on Sidney Umsted's oil wells.

Success (Clay): When Bridgeport was bypassed by the St. Louis, Iron Mountain and Southern Railroad, residents established a new town on the railroad in 1895 and gave it an optimistic but otherwise unexplained name. Deane surmises it was because of the town's successful move.

Sulphur City (Washington): Donald Harrington sorted through conflicting chronologies and says that the town was first called New Prospect. Then, in 1876, the new post office was called Mankins for postmaster Peter Mankins. In order to attract tourists, residents decided to rename it Sulphur Springs, but the USPS refused this, and Mankins himself nixed retaining the current name, so the residents finally settled on Sulphur City.

Sulphur Springs (Yell): A health resort of the early nineteenth century, which included the springs all under one roof, it was also called the Dardanelle Sulphur Springs, and the post office was established in 1879.

Turrell *TUHR-uhl* (Crittenden): The settlement grew up in the 1880s around the lumber company owned by Fletcher E. Turrell.

Twist (Cross): Early in the twentieth century, Ira F. Twist and his son, Frank, established a sharecropping operation that would eventually encompass twenty-one thousand acres.

Victoria (Mississippi): Established as a company town in the 1880s by Robert E. Lee Wilson to support loggers and sharecroppers and named for his sister.

West Memphis (Crittenden): Deane writes that the settlement formed shortly before World War I was built around a logging camp and sawmill owned by Zack Bragg, and so it was originally called Bragg or Bragg's Spur. The name was changed in 1927 in hopes of cashing in on foreign markets wanting lumber from the famous city across the river.

West Point (White): Not a directional name but established in 1850 as a port on the Little Red River by businessman J.M. West, who picked the name.

Wilson (Mississippi): One of the company towns built by Robert E. Lee Wilson for his lumber workers and sharecroppers.

Wing (Yell): The town was originally called Fair Hill in honor of a beloved pastor, Nathan Hill, but after the Wing Construction Company set up shop in the 1880s, it was renamed.

Zinc (Boone): Established around 1900 to serve local zinc mines.

Chapter 8

CURIOUS AND CURIOUSER

Besides the usual categories of place names, Arkansas has a remarkable number of names that elude explanation. Many towns have legendary explanations for their names, some of which may be true but most of which are probably based on either wild surmise or stories handed down from residents whose memories were of varying degrees of reliability. And finally, there are all those towns whose names have no known origin stories. While most of those are not listed herein, there are some that absolutely demand some kind of explanation, truthful or not.

Alma *ALE-muh* (Crawford): The "Spinach Capital of the World" was originally called Gum Town or Gumtown because of the numerous sweet gum trees, many of which were used to make log cabins. There are competing stories about how the name was selected in 1872. Some say Alma was the sweetheart of a nearby postmaster, and some say the name was drawn from a hat. One resident recalled that "Alma was almost forced upon us in order to secure a certificate from the postmaster of Van Buren…who claimed the right to name the town." One last tale says that in a meeting where each person present wrote down a name, there was a tie vote between two names, and a small group settled on Alma. A lot of stories for a four-letter name.

Amity (Clark): The town was settled in the 1840s and named by an early settler (either William F. Browning or Dr. Amariah Biggs) in hopes of "peace and brotherhood," perhaps from the Old French *amitié*.

Antoine *ann-TOYN* (Pike): The town was built on the Antoine River, which allegedly got its romantic name from a French trapper whose corpse was found at his camp nearby and whose only identification gave his name as "Antoine." The area around his grave became the town cemetery, but the tombstone, if it ever existed, is long gone.

Arkadelphia *ARK-uh-DEL-fee-uh*: Clark County seat, called Blakeytown until 1839, according to legend, for Adam Blakeley. The current name is a puzzler: the best guesses are that the "Ark" is for Arkansas, or perhaps for "arc of," and *adelphos* is Greek, for "brother." Or perhaps it's simply copying the town of the same name in Alabama.

Athens (Howard): Established after the Civil War by Daniel Baber but allegedly so named by a Professor Amos from Athens, Greece.

Auvergne *aw-VERN* (Jackson): Settled after the Civil War and originally called Sand Hill; the name was changed in 1882. According to one story, this was the name of founder James T. Henderson's farm. A second story says that in his rush to come up with a name for the post office application, the storekeeper/postmaster took it from a bag of flour. The third story, or perhaps a version of the first, says that it was Henderson's wife who came up with the name, from either a French novel or the name on a barrel of flour.

Avoca *uh-VOHK-uh* (Benton): Established as a stop on a stagecoach route and originally called Brightwater or Bestwater, for nearby Sugar Creek's clear water. It was later renamed by store owner Albert Peel, "probably for the river and town" in Ireland. Another story says that Peel heard a poem recited by a railroad worker, "The Meeting of the Waters" by Thomas Moore, which mentions "the sweet vale of Avoca."

Barber (Logan): Established in Scott County around 1869, and the post office existed from 1878 until 1979. An exceedingly unlikely story credits the name to "Uncle Doss Peoples," who as a boy used to chant, "Send for the barber." When the railroad bypassed the town, the residents moved from the north side of Big Washburn Creek to the south side. The town became part of Logan County in 1903.

Belleville (Yell): A sawmill town called Ferguson Springs or Ferguson Mills, named for the first postmaster, was settled in the 1870s. But when the railroad depot was built a mile away, most of the residents moved there in 1899. There are two stories for the current name: first, the city had many beautiful girls, and second, Belle Starr was a frequent visitor to the town. But since Starr died ten years before the founding of the new town, that story seems just a bit implausible.

Ben Hur (Newton): Until Newton County was formed around 1930 and included the town, it was in Pope County. It was one of at least five towns in the United States (the others are in California, Florida, Virginia and Texas) named for the novel by Lew Wallace and the last town in Arkansas to get electricity, which finally arrived in 1969.

Ben Lomond *BEN LOH-mun* (Sevier): Settled in the middle of the nineteenth century and named for either a mountain or a loch in Scotland, depending on who's telling the story.

Berlin *BURR-linn* (Ashley): Established in the 1850s, and since two of the first merchants had German Jewish names, its name obviously references the city in Germany.

Billstown (Pike): Established in the last half of the nineteenth century and first called Pleasant Hill. There are two stories as to how it got the name. One says it was because there were several settlers named William. (*See also* Johnsville.) A second tale says it was named for shopkeeper Bill Thompson.

Birdell *buhr-DELL* (Randolph): Named by Joseph Hufstedler for his two daughters, Birdie and Ella.

Birdeye (Cross): At first called Walnut Camp, but this changed, for reasons that remain speculative. One story, often told, says that on a map, the town is no bigger than a bird's eye. Others say that—but not why—the name was given by Blacks. Neither tale passes muster.

Blackville (Jackson): One historian speculates that the post office was so named because most of the patrons were Black.

Bloomer (Sebastian): Settled in the mid-nineteenth century and with a lively variety of tales about its name, gathered by the industrious Deane: (1) Some travelers sighted a pair of bloomers hanging out on a line, but how those travelers influenced the naming process is unclear; (2) It was named for an early settler named Bloomer; and (3) The name is a variant of "boomer," contemporary slang for a migratory worker...because towns are routinely named with slang insults? The second of these seems the least egregious.

Blue Ball (Scott): Settled in the middle of the nineteenth century. Resident Salina Millard is said to have awakened one cold morning and exclaimed that the mountain outside looked like a blue ball. Deane relates that Millard heard a neighbor make that comment. Both stories seem suspect.

Blue Eye (Carroll): Originally called Butler's Barrens and ostensibly renamed for the eyes of early settler Elbert Butler, or those of his daughter. Straddling the line with Missouri, this is the northernmost and smallest incorporated area in Arkansas.

Board Camp (Polk): There is a story about a family that hunkered down in the early nineteenth century to wait out some illness. Instead of using logs to build their cabin, they dressed the logs into boards. After the family left, hunters used the building, which they called "that board camp," which was the name given in the 1878 post office application.

Boston, town (Madison) and a range of mountains: The town was probably named for the Massachusetts city, but the mountains are less certain. Perhaps their name is a corruption of a French phrase for "rough road," or related to the American western slang term "a Boston," meaning anything particularly difficult. Deane notes that French *bosse* can mean an elevated surface, so your hill would be *bosse ton*, which seems strained.

Bright Star (Howard): This Black community at one time had two churches, a school and a lovely if mysteriously given name.

Brightstar (Miller): In one of Deane's livelier tales, the town of Stuckeyville, originally named for the Stuckey family, was renamed owing to a drunken traveler proclaiming how bright the stars were and that the place should be named "Bright Star." This is another entry on the list of "names from travelers," but with the twist of this traveler being inebriated.

Brown Springs (Hot Springs): While the origins of the name are undiscovered, its history has been lively. In the 1950s, when Highway 51 was paved, the new signs from the Highway Commission proclaimed that the community was now Faber, just as the commission had changed the name of nearby Bethlehem to Joan. The town's residents, however, campaigned successfully to have the name reset to Brown Springs.

Budd Kidd Creek (Washington): Originally called Bob Kidd Creek for a popular Black man and his family, but the Highway Department changed the name on a road sign.

Buffalo City (Baxter): Located where the Buffalo River empties into the White River, and probably as far upstream as paddle wheelers could go. The town straddles the White River, with Old Buffalo City on the western side and New on the east bank.

Bug Scuffle Church (Washington): Deane relates a tale of a boring preacher and men waiting outside the church taking bets on the outcome of a fight between two tumblebugs competing for a bit of manure. And no, says Deane, the men never did go back inside the church.

Bullfrog Valley (Pope): Notorious in the late nineteenth century as a hideout for moonshiners, highwaymen and forgers, this area was allegedly named for Chief Bullfrog, in legend a Cherokee whose people settled there after their march on the Trail of Tears from Georgia around 1830.

Butter Creek (Van Buren): A tall tale says that a local farmer made butter by pouring milk into the creek, where the rocks would churn it.

Buttermilk (Pope): Deane recounts a tale of how during a rainstorm, the whitewash came off the walls of the church, as if it had been painted with buttermilk. He wisely doesn't try to explain how such an unlikely story could lead to a town's name.

Buttermilk Spring (Benton): Originally a stagecoach stop that was known for the widow who sold five-cent cups of buttermilk to passengers.

Calion *KALE-yuhn* (Union): Since it is just across the Ouachita River from Calhoun County, the name given in 1912 combines the first three letters of Calhoun and the final three of Union.

Camp (Fulton): Settled early in the nineteenth century and named Indian Camp, allegedly because of Native Americans living nearby. By the time the post office was established in 1884, the name had been shortened to Camp.

Casa *KAY-suh* (Perry): While the town was settled in the 1830s, it was not incorporated until 1900. The name, says a lovely tale, was given by "a Spanish family" because the town was so homelike, but apparently not homelike enough for them to remain.

Cash (Craighead): Established on a small railroad between Bono and the Cache River around 1900 and named Soonover, some say because it was not expected to last long. When it did endure, it was later renamed for the Cache River.

Center Point (Howard): Formed in the middle of the nineteenth century and named for its hoped-for role as a central location for trade in southwestern Arkansas. It is a neat coincidence that it is also at the center of Howard County, which was formed later, but the town did serve as a convenient location for the county seat for many years.

Centerton (Benton): The Arkansas-Oklahoma Railroad established a depot in 1900 near the Center Point Methodist Church and school, so named for being in the center of the county. But since there was already a Center Point in Howard County, the post office was named Centerton.

Chute Rock (Madison): This town got its name when part of the hillside became the top portion of a chute constructed by loggers to slide logs down to wagons below, and the name stuck.

Clay County: Established in 1873 and named for John M. Clayton, a state senator and brother of Powell Clayton, a Republican Reconstruction governor who declared martial law in that part of the state and forbid residents from participating in the 1868 elections. The name was changed in 1875 on a petition from a local attorney. While the attorney's clear aim was to expunge any association with the Republican governor, he disingenuously claimed that it was to honor Henry Clay.

Collegeville (Saline): An unincorporated community, it was founded, designed and named in 1827 by Ezra Owen from Virginia, who hoped it would become the capital of Arkansas and the home of the first state college. The town was first called Dogwood Springs, but Owen changed the name to be more clear about the town's purpose. Now it is largely part of Bryant.

Congo (Saline): Established in the mid-nineteenth century but not named until 1893. After the Post Office rejected two proposed names, so says the story, a prominent citizen's daughter who had been studying Africa in school suggested "Congo." The Post Office approved this name in 1893, but the story is highly suspect.

Cow Faced Hill (Benton): Among the more unlikely tales related by Deane is one of a man frightened by a ghost one night near the site of a murder. In the light of day, he realized he had been frightened by a white-faced cow, and thus the name.

Croker (Izard): A railroad station, established about 1904, was called Croker Spur, possibly—if implausibly—because of the bullfrogs along the river. In 1924, the post office took that name, and the "Spur" was dropped in 1933.

Dalark *DAL-ark* (Dallas and Clark Counties): A nice portmanteau of both county names.

Danville: One of two seats of Yell County, it was settled in the 1840s and named by founder John B. Howell for the steamboat, *Danville*, that he had previously captained.

Dardanelle: The other Yell County seat's post office was established in 1823. Goodspeed speculates romantically, if unrealistically, that the three-hundred-foot-high rock face by the river might have reminded David Brearley, an Indian agent who had purchased the land, of the Dardanelles in Turkey. Another story has Brearly being shown the area by a French trader who called the bluff "the Dardonnie," which, along with the resemblance to the Turkish site, persuaded Brearly to so name it. Goodspeed also gives a cock-and-bull story about the rocks being used as lookout posts by Indians, whose word for sleeping with one eye open was *dandonnie*, noting an 1809 report giving Dardi as the bluff's name. The most romantic story, rightly regarded as sentimental bosh, recounts the star-crossed tale of Indian boy Dard and girl Nell, whose tribes were at war. In their attempt to be together, both youth were lost in the river,

Delight. *Courtesy of Jimmy Emerson, DVM.*

which tragedy helped to reconcile the tribes. Almost certainly, the town was named for Jean Baptist Dardenne, a French coureur de bois with a large Spanish land grant, who went to court to prove his claim.

Deer (Newton): The town was established in 1898 and, according to the local story, named for a pet deer owned by E.B. Jones, which "ran in the woods with his cows at that time." The team name for the nearby high school is the Antlers.

Delight *duh-LITE* (Pike): Settled in the early nineteenth century, the town was incorporated in 1904 when Dr. William Kirkham was assigned to name the town, which he said was a delightful place to live.

Des Arc: One of two seats of Prairie County, settled in the late eighteenth century and taking its name from the nearby Bayou des Arc or des Arcs. How the bayou got its name is more contentious: Deane says it was because the bayou was curved, but others argue that "Arcs" is an abbreviation of Arcansas, as in Poste des Arcs (Arkansas Post) or Aux Arcs. Early versions of the town and bayou's names include d'Arc, Des Ark, des Arques, Desarc, Des Arcs Bluff and Dezark Bluff, as well as McNulty's Bluff and Francisville.

DeView (Woodruff): One local belief is that the name is owing to a nice view; another attributes it to bison, as in *veau*, "calf"; but neither is convincing.

Devils Den (Washington): Deane relates a tale of early settlers hearing "the roar of the Devil" from a number of caves in the area, now a state park. There are Devils Dens in other states, and all seem to have distinctive stories about their names.

Dexter (Jefferson): Deane relates the tale of a community founder naming the town for his horse Dexter, a most excellent tale.

Dorcheat Bayou (Columbia): An 1806 explorer said that the Caddo called this bayou Datche, meaning "a gap eaten by a bear in a log," which is a marvelous if unbelievable explanation. Scholars once thought that the name might mean "people" in Caddo. Deane speculates that Dorcheat may be a French revision of the Caddo word, or perhaps it was originally known as the Bayu Daicet.

Drasco (Cleburne): Settled in the mid-nineteenth century and called Crossroads or Cross Roads until 1917. The town was seeking a post office, and the USPS required that a new name be provided. The postmistress submitted the name Drasco, supposedly a branch of the Blackfoot Indians, but this is rubbish as there is no evidence of such a people and the Blackfoot Indians had never lived anywhere near the area, so another story is needed.

Driftwood (Lawrence): Emancipated slaves settled the area after the Civil War, and the town existed well into the twentieth century. Legend says it was named for the former slaves and other African Americans who just "drifted" into the area.

Dutch Creek (Yell): Allsopp says, quite unbelievably—and his tale gained traction—that the town was named for an Indian chief. Perhaps "Dutch" was a transliteration of some other word.

El Dorado: *el dor-RAY-doe*: The seat of Union County was founded and named in 1843, according to legend, because original store owner Matthew Rainey found business to be so good. Deane relates the unlikely tale that it was because of a common greeting: wagon trains asked each other, "Where is your El Dorado?" Allsopp poetically speculates that "the musical sound of the name may have appealed to the romantic natures of the pioneers, whose lives for the most part were full of trials and hardships." Perhaps the most likely, if still unsatisfactory, story is that inside his store, Rainy operated the El Dorado Bar.

Elevenpoint (Randolph): Settled in the late nineteenth century on the east bank of the Elevenpoint River. The first post office opened in 1911, named Cavenar after the postmaster, and the name was changed in 1915 to Elevenpoint. Branner suggests that the name of the river comes from *leve pont*, or "elevated bridge." Others, noting that this word order is incorrect, can only weakly speculate that eleven creeks empty into the river.

Enola *in-OH-luh* (Faulkner): A lost traveler, according to legend, in despair carved onto some wood the word *alone*. In the 1840s, someone from the new town found the carving, inexplicably read it backwards and so named the town. Or perhaps the "lost traveler" carved it backwards, so profound was his despair. In any case, more likely is the tale of a little girl named Enola Miller. Less reliable is the story of a chapter of the Grange named Enola Grange No. 142 in Mount Vernon that eventually moved to the town.

Enon *EE-nuhn* (Drew): A local story says that the town was settled in the mid-nineteenth century and first called Old Smokey, allegedly from a name for the wood-fired cotton gin, or because of the Smoky Mountains. A local story says that the name is just the reverse of "None." There is no word on whether any of these stories also apply to the 1901 town of Enon in Carroll County.

Etowah *ET-uh-waw* (Mississippi): Around 1900, a settlement grew up to support a lumber mill. The original name, Jackson's Island, was rejected by the USPS, and the inexplicable Etowah got the nod. The story is that an American Indian rode through the area shouting "Etowah!" but the word has no meaning in any known language. Deane, surmising that the Indian was drunk, suggests he was referring to his Cherokee home in Georgia.

Eureka Springs: One of the two seats of Carroll County, long famous for the sixty-two hot springs in the town. When the town was named around 1880, the name Eureka, Greek for "I have found [it]," was selected, perhaps on the basis of a tale that credited the exclamation to Ponce de Leon having there located the Fountain of Youth. A great story, except that he never found the fountain and Spanish sailors seldom conversed in Classical Greek.

Evening Shade (Cleburne): An improvement on the former name, Nigger Hill.

Evening Shade (Scott): Settled in the 1830s, and one story says that the original church, built at the foot of Poteau Mountain, was shaded after three o'clock in the afternoon and so took on the name. Similarly implausible is the tale that early residents used to wait in the shade of the plum trees for the deer to come to the spring.

Evening Shade (Sharp): Established in the early nineteenth century and known first as Hook Rum and then Shanty, eventually being named— presumably—for the shade offered by a stand of pine trees near the downtown. The seat of Sharp County from 1868 until 1963.

Farewell (Carroll): When a schoolhouse built in 1870 was being replaced by a better building, says the tale, town residents debated long but fruitlessly about a new name. Finally, someone complained about the late hour of the meeting and said, "I'm going home. Farewell to you." Sometimes spelled Farwell.

Fifty-Six (Stone): The town was originally called Newcomb, but in 1918 the USPS rejected this proposed name. Postmaster Reid W. Newcomb said that he chose the name Fifty-Six (with or without the hyphen) because that was the number of the school district.

Figure Five (Crawford): A marvelous tale says that surveyor James Graham Stevenson, who had determined that the location was five miles from Van Buren, carved a 5 into a tree trunk and wrote to his family telling them to settle near the tree. Another legend says that Stevenson was on a cattle drive and carved the numeral to mark that they had covered about five miles that day. In any event, no matter why he carved the 5, Stevenson's family didn't settle there.

Fly Gap (Franklin): This gap through the Boston Mountains was infamous for the swarms of flies drawn to all the moonshine stills in the area.

Forty Four (Izard): A community grew up around a lumber mill in the 1880s, and the reasonably probable story is that during a fruitless discussion to come up with a name, someone noted that the petition to get a post office had forty-four names.

Forum (Madison): Yet another story of a community meeting unable to decide on a name until someone pointed out that they composed a forum and wouldn't that be a good name?

Friendship (Hot Spring): The early settlers in the 1850s apparently enjoyed each other's company.

Gainesville (Greene): The small town was so named, says a truly dubious story, because in the 1840s "it gained the county seat."

Gassville (Baxter): Established in the mid-nineteenth century on a bend in the White River and so known first as Turkey's Neck. When its post office was established in 1878, the town took on a name that launched a cottage industry of etymologies. One local legend says that the town was named for the first postmaster, Pinkney A. Cox, whose verbosity made him known as a "gasser." Deane recounts another cock-and-bull story about how Cox was a practical joker. Once, after natural gas was discovered nearby, "Pinky" surreptitiously poured some gas into a cistern and proved his claim that there was gas by tossing in a burning stick. A third story credits railroad workers regularly "gassing" around the campfire at night.

Gateway (Benton): This town is on the border with Missouri, so many suppose that this is the origin of the name. In fact, it was named for an arch over Highway 62 that said it was the "Gateway to Eureka Springs."

Gepp *Jeep* (Fulton): Deane says that a first application in 1946 for a post office named Plainview was rejected, and a postal official suggested Jeep, perhaps to commemorate the vehicle's service in World War II. Thereupon the USPS either misspelled it as Jepp or there already was a Jepp and the spelling was changed to Gepp. In any case, the name has always been pronounced *Jeep*.

Glen Rose (Hot Spring): In 1927, says one story, a salesman visiting the local country school and discovering that the town had no name suggested

Glen Rose School. *Author's collection.*

Glen Rose because of the rosebushes at the school. The second story says that it was named for University of Arkansas basketball and football coach Glen Rose, who was at UA off and on from 1933 to 1966.

Glenwood (Pike): The town was platted in 1907 near a railroad depot and called Holly, perhaps for the bushes. When the USPS denied this name in 1910, a real estate broker came up with Glenwood, no doubt hopeful that it would attract clients.

Granny's Gap (Pope): Deane relates one of those bogus "named by a visitor" legends: the settlement was named for an elderly lady spending the night on her trip through the gap in the mountains.

Greasy Corner (St. Francis): Often on lists of unusual place names and with good reason and an excellent story. This spot in the road was originally named Mack's Corner for local landowner B.M. McCollum. McCollum operated a restaurant and automobile shop in the same building, which astonishingly resulted in less-than-hygienic conditions. One day, when an auto mechanic (doubling as a waiter) served a local farmer a plate of food stained with automobile grease, the customer called out to McCollum and exclaimed that "the town should be called Greasy Corner." And so, in keeping with other "exclamation" stories, it was.

Greasy Creek (Madison): The home of Governor Orval Faubus sadly lacks a story for its name.

Greasy Valley (Van Buren): To make up for Greasy Creek, this has three stories. In one, it was named by Indians "because of the greasy scum found on most of the springs," which is surely bogus. Another story says it was called this by White settlers because of the many fat bears and other wildlife. A third and more likely tale is that before farmers had fenced in their properties, many allowed their hogs to forage in the woods, and it was the abundance of these acorn-fed hogs that led to the name.

Greensboro (Craighead): Established in the early nineteenth century, the 1842 post office was named Delaware Hill. Early blacksmith George Gregson, who had come from Greensboro, North Carolina, was most likely the source of the new name. Or perhaps—although this seems exceedingly unlikely—because it was on the road to Greene County, the name was changed to Greensborough in 1850 and later shortened to the current form.

Hasty (Newton): Established about 1902, the town was originally called Gum Tavern or Agee, after early settler John Agee. In the 1880s, says one local history, "a fast inflow of settlers" led postmistress Joanna Morrison to ask for the name Hasty Ridge, and the post office name later dropped the "Ridge."

Health (Washington): Deane relates a tale of postmaster John S. Brannon, seeking relief from low country malaria and naming his mountain settlement in Madison County either Health or Helth.

Hector (Pope): Perhaps unmatched among Arkansas places for the tale behind its name. Although the town was originally called The Plain, postmaster Henry Jefferson Mayo unilaterally decided to make his 1888 post office application for the name Avondale, for his Indiana hometown— but, oddly, only on a six-month trial basis. This seems characteristic of the increasingly unpopular Mayo, and angry residents petitioned for another name. And there were many proposals, including Snider (for a local physician); Wheeler, Wootenville and Grindersville after early settlers; and Greenville for local tanner Green Caudle, who was at least more popular than Mayo. Finally, the town agreed on Greensville, but the USPS, sick of the bickering, apparently—if implausibly—wrote to the White House and asked President Grover Cleveland for a name. He picked Hector, the name of his favorite dog. All of which finally persuaded Mayo to leave town, so at least there was one positive outcome.

Herbine Hunting Club. *Author's collection.*

Herbine *HER-bean* (Cleveland): When the post office opened in 1906, the first suggested name, Crook, was—not surprisingly—rejected. Local legend, with some variants, says that during the ensuing discussion in J.O. Crook's general store, a group selected the name of a patent medicine on Crook's shelf.

Hogeye or **Hog Eye** (Washington): Interestingly, the town discarded the early name of Moffit, as found on maps from around 1900, in favor of this, with a variety of explanations. Some involve fiddlers, including a gypsy fiddler asked to play "Hawk Eye" but thinking it was "Hog Eye," or an itinerant fiddler playing for liquor who replayed the same tune, "Hog Eye," without stop. Are we to believe that the residents thought naming the town after the song would shut up the fiddler? Some say, with admirable imagination, that the town was so small it was "no bigger than a hog's eye," a unit of measurement not much used now. Most likely, the name is a corruption of biblical Haggai, which is still an interesting tale.

Hogscald Hollow (Carroll): Folktales tell of basins in a creek in the Ozarks used by either local residents or Union soldiers for scalding hog carcasses before butchering.

Hominy (Hempstead): A wonderful name, but not related to ground corn. It was originally Harmony, but the spelling eventually matched up with the pronunciation.

Hookrum (Sharp): Deane provides one of his more detailed and unlikely tales. He says that this nickname for Evening Shade was allegedly owing to an unpopular farmer who, while at cards, was plied with rum and then lost his money. He stood on a counter waving his empty glass and yelling that he had been given rum and hooked of his money: "Hookrum, hookrum, hookrum." This story clearly needs work.

Horsehead Creek (Johnson): A local tale says that early settlers found the large head of a horse impaled on a pole.

Humnoke *HUM-uh-noke* (Lonoke): Founded early in the twentieth century, halfway between Humphrey and Lonoke, from which two towns the name derives.

Huntsville: The seat of Madison County was settled around 1827. Although many of the first residents came from Tennessee, some from Alabama got the settlement named for their hometown.

Iceledo (Newton): Deane relates the tale of a resident coming up with this name because the town was so isolated, a story as sad as it is unbelievable.

Ico *EYE-koh* (Grant): Called Wardsville before 1886, after which the name's history becomes speculation. One story says that the town was named for the W.C. Osborne family and another that Ico was named for "nothing in particular."

Independence County: Named in honor of the Declaration of Independence.

Indian Bay (Monroe): Near the bayou of Turk Bay, a town was laid out in 1836 and first called New Warsaw and also Bay Town. By 1860, the post office was called Indian Bay, the name that became accepted and so incorporated in 1876, with no record of exactly why. Allsopp says it was because the Cherokee loved the area and notes a large Indian mound nearby, which has been identified as Quapaw.

Ink (Polk): There are a number of variations on the tale of this name. The most well known says that when residents were asked to suggest a name on the post office application, they took literally the instructions to "write in ink." Deane alters this to say that the local schoolmarm told her neighbors to "write in ink," which many of them did. A less credible tale says that the postmistress at the time of application, in the list of suggested names, jokingly wrote "Inky," which the post office accepted and shortened to Ink.

Jacksonport (Jackson): The first seat of Jackson County was established in the 1840s at the confluence of the White and Black Rivers, and one local story says that it was named for Jackson County in Tennessee. Later, residents refused the railroad's request for a $25,000 grant to build the line through their town, which thereupon dwindled, and the county seat was moved to Newport.

Jasper: The seat of Newton County was established in 1840, and there are three stories, all fairly sketchy, for the name. First, it was so named by Cherokees on the Trail of Tears who were surprised by the warm hospitality of the village, which is lovely, even if it doesn't explain anything. Second, as a variant of the first, a precious ring—presumably with a jasper—was given to the postmaster by Chief John Ross in gratitude for the care given to the Cherokees. And third, postmaster John Ross compared the color of the local stone, a block of which had been sent to Washington, D.C., in 1836 for the Washington Monument, to the jewel mentioned in Revelations. Local historians continue to disagree. For his part, Deane notes that some cities with this name were named for Sergeant Jasper of Revolutionary War fame and that Jasper, Minnesota, seems to have been named for nearby reddish rocks.

Jericho (Crittenden): Some of the 1840s founders are said to have come from near Jericho, Pennsylvania, and Jericho, South Carolina, but probably none from the city in Palestine.

Joan *JOE-ann* (Clark): The town was settled in the 1850s around Bethlehem Methodist Church and, logically, known as Bethlehem for a century. In the mid-1950s, after Highway 51 had been paved, the Arkansas Highway Commission erected signs informing drivers that they were entering Joan, which was a great surprise to the residents, who had never heard of this name. Confronted by this fait accompli, the residents adjusted to their new name. *See also* Brown Springs for a community with a similar story, albeit a different ending.

Kings River (Madison and Carroll Counties): According to legend, the river is named for prospector Henry King, who explored the area in 1827. This is contradicted by an 1823 newspaper article referring to the Kings River.

Knoxville (Johnson): Established in 1873 when the Little Rock & Fort Smith built a depot on land owned by Thomas May, who had named a small settlement Mayville. The depot itself was called Black Fox or Black Rock. When the town had grown enough for a post office, the name Mayville was rejected, so May named it for the town in Tennessee that had probably been his home.

Kokomo (Lee): Originally a railroad spur and one of many towns in America with this name. Deane attributes it to the suggestion of a logger from that town in Indiana who was working the area around 1915. This seems unlikely, but there has been no other theory put forth.

Laconia Circle (Desha): While there is no written evidence, the town's name is surely from the Greek home state of Sparta.

Lamartine (Columbia): Settled in the mid-nineteenth century and believed to have been named by early settler John Dockery for contemporary French poet and politician Alphonse Marie Louis de Prat de Lamartine.

Lepanto *lee-PANT-oh* (Poinsett): This town was originally called Potter's Landing when it was settled in the 1870s. The U.S. Post Office asked for a different name in 1894. Local history says that the Post Office selected this name from the submissions, presumably for the great naval battle, and it is the only Lepanto in the United States.

Little Africa (Lawrence): Settled after the Civil War by formerly enslaved persons on the Strawberry River, near the confluence with the Black, the town disappeared about 1925. A similarly named town in Polk County was abandoned around 1910 after a lynching in Mena.

Little Texas (Scott): In 1870, migrants from Mississippi on a wagon train bound for Texas decided it had gone far enough, stopped and established the town.

Lost Bridge (Benton): A bridge was being constructed in the 1920s over the White River, but funding dried up with the Great Depression, and it was never completed. A flood in 1943 washed away the frame, and when Beaver Lake was made, the ruins were covered by two hundred feet of water. A community on Beaver Lake was established with this lovely name in 1967.

Lost Corner (Conway): According to Deane, the settlement originally had the wonderful name of Okay. When the USPS balked at this name because there was another Okay, postmaster George Napier came up with this acknowledgement of the town's isolation.

Loyal (Independence): A community so named because it stayed loyal to the Union in the Civil War.

Malvern: The seat of Hot Spring County was founded in the 1870s as a railroad station and supposed to have been named by a native Virginian who said it reminded him of his home area, the Civil War battlefield of Malvern Hill. Another quite old story claims that it was named after a railroad worker named John Malvern.

Manila (Mississippi): Established in the late nineteenth century and first called Cinda, after Lucinda, the postmaster's sister. When the town was incorporated in 1901, the residents voted to name it in honor of Commodore George Dewey's Spanish-American War victory in Manila Bay. Some of the streets were named for battleships that had been engaged in the battle.

Mansfield (Sebastian and Scott Counties): Established in 1888, merging two superbly named towns, Coop Prairie and Chocoville, at a depot on the Little Rock & Texas Railroad. There are two stories for the name. The line surveyor is supposed to have officially reported that the track had got as far as "some man's field," and the name stuck. Far more probably, the town was named for Arkansas Supreme Court justice William W. Mansfield, although the "man's field" tale has some sympathetic partisans still.

Marcella (Stone): Settled by the Hess Family in the early nineteenth century and first called Hess Town. In 1880, so says the story, Thomas Hess picked the name Marcella because he liked it.

Marche *mar-SHAY* (Pulaski): The town of Bartlett was established in 1866 but essentially wiped out by cholera in 1872. Immigrant Poles were lured by the Little Rock & Fort Smith Railroad to take up residence in the town. In

1879, they named their new town Warren but had to change that because of the Bradley County town of the same name. Deane rues that "why the name, which means market in French, was selected appears unknown."

Marion: The seat of Crittenden County was established early in the nineteenth century with a name that defies explanation. One story says it was named for Marion Tolbert, a county commissioner who gave land for the city. Another version alleges there is no record that Tolbert was named Marion and suggests it was named for a town in Crittenden County, Kentucky, whence came some settlers.

Marked Tree (Poinsett): This was a landing site on the Little River in the early nineteenth century and named for a tree on the bank that had a large *M* carved on it. One really curious story says that the *M* was carved by "a wiley old Indian chief named Moonshine," which is as delightful as it is entirely bogus. More likely is the legend that the *M* was carved by the notorious outlaw John Murrell to mark a rendezvous in his trading of stolen horses and enslaved persons. The place served as a camp for workers on the Kansas City, Fort Scott and Gulf Railroad, but an 1890

Marked Tree. *Courtesy of the Library of Congress Prints and Photographs Division.*

flood finally washed away the tree, the rendezvous and all recorded history of wily Chief Moonshine.

Martin Box (Searcy): Deane relates the long-standing if utterly nonsensical tale of residents constructing a small school building and a traveler stopping to ask if they were building a martin box.

Maumelle: The Maumelle and the Little Maumelle Rivers flow out of the Ouachita National Forest into the Arkansas River near the community of Maumelle. Lonely French explorers in the early nineteenth century, gazing at the rock formation now called Pinnacle Mountain, saw it as shaped like a breast and so named it Mamelle.

Mayflower (Faulkner): Established as a railroad telegraph station around 1871 during railroad construction. Deane confidently asserts that the railroad supervisor used the name of his Pullman car as his address. Another version of the tale says that the telegraph operator used "Mayflower" as his telegraph call sign, and so the name stuck. There is no known documentary evidence for either story.

Mazarn, Montgomery County town and mountain: The town was a going concern by the mid-nineteenth century. Deane suggests that the name, which was also spelled "Musserne," was an evolution from French Mont Cerne (round mountain).

Melbourne: The seat of Izard County was established in 1854 and first called Mill Creek. The new name, thought to mean "mill stream," was selected by W.C. Dixon in 1876. Whether Dixon wanted to honor the Australian city or he just liked the sound is not known.

Millwood (Phillips): Deane relates the local tradition that the name came not, as one might reasonably guess, from a sawmill but from the label of a popular brand of whiskey.

Moark *MOH-ark* (Clark): The name of the little town cleverly combines the postal abbreviations of two states, although why Missouri instead of the much closer Louisiana or Oklahoma remains a mystery.

Moccasin Gap (Pope): Deane can find nothing better than some cock-and-bull story of an old (unnamed) chief of an (unnamed) Indian tribe, who, when forced to relocate, burned his moccasins in protest. His gesture, unsurprisingly, seems to have been ineffective.

Moko (Fulton): Received wisdom relates that the 1901 application for a post office originally sought the name "Golden," but at some point in the process, and with no explanation, this name was crossed out and "Moko" was written in.

Monette *moh-NET* (Craighead): Established on the line of the Jonesboro, Lake City and Eastern Railroad. One story says it was named for the wife or two daughters (Mona and Nettie) of a railroad executive, but there is no documentary evidence of that. More mundanely, it might have been named for Monette, Missouri, or Monette, Mississippi.

Monkey Run (Baxter): The settlement that grew up in the 1870s around Pilgrim's Rest Baptist Church was, logically, first called Pilgrim's Rest. Its wonderful current name has four stories to explain it, of which three involve a local shopkeeper. In the first, he is rudely awakened by a group of boys and chases them away, yelling, "Watch them monkeys run." In the second, it is the boys who dare each other to "watch that old monkey run" and chase them. In the third, more dignified if less logical, the shopkeeper has bought so many gifts for his sweetheart that he needs to make many trips to the city in order to restock his merchandise, and the locals say, "There goes the old monkey on his run." A fourth legend is a somewhat more credible tale of an early settler's pet monkey that ran away. Later attempts by the town merchants to change the name back to Pilgrim's Rest failed. One local history says that the town was founded on the crossroads at Monkey Run Creek but doesn't say whether the creek's name or the town's came first.

Monticello *MON-tuh-SEL-loe or MON-tuh-SEL-luh*: The seat of Drew County was originally settled in the 1830s about two miles south of the current location and called Rough and Ready, probably in honor of President Zachary Taylor. When the town moved north in 1849 to the new location, it was most likely renamed in honor of the estate of Thomas Jefferson, with the pronunciation changed a bit from the Italian.

Montrose *MAHN-trohz* (Ashley): A railroad depot of the Iron Mountain Railroad, named, according to Deane, by the founder of a nearby mill who had come from Montrose, Colorado, where there really is a mountain.

Moreland (Pope): Deane relates a tale of a stagecoach passenger coming over Gravel Hill remarking that "we're going to need more land," a tale which is so contrived and so unbelievable that it must almost certainly be true.

Morning Star: There are two such towns in Arkansas. The one in Searcy County was named to match up with nearby Evening Star, while there is no known story behind the name of the town that straddles the Hot Spring-Garland county line.

Mound City (Crittenden): Allsopp records that this had been a population center for Indigenous people, and the White settlement was so named for all of the nearby Indian mounds.

Mountain Home: The name of the Baxter County seat has had an interesting history. It was originally called Rapp's Barren or sometimes Talbert's Barren, which was not a pejorative term at the time. In Appalachian English, "barrens" referred to places that had been cleared for agricultural use by burning, often regularly. Rapp was the nickname of an early settler, Walter Talbert. In fact, one of his nephews was named Rapp in honor of his uncle. Pretty quickly, the residents became aware that calling a place barren was not especially great for civic promotion, and the 1857 post office was allegedly named for how enslaved persons, traveling up from their plantations in the low country, referred to their upcountry plantations as "My Sweet Mountain Home," one of the state's most dubious tales.

Mount Ida: The seat of Montgomery County was established in 1842 and, logically, first called Montgomery. In 1850, it became Salem and then Mount Ida, allegedly because the founder's former home near Boston, Massachusetts, had been so named.

Mount Pleasant (Izard): The town, established after the Civil War in what was then Independence County, was originally called Barren Fork, ostensibly for the nearby creek. Its unfortunate nickname of Dry Town was owing, according to one story, to the town's wells regularly going dry in the summer.

Allsopp, curiously, says it was because of the distance to the nearest creek, which would contradict the official name. In any case, Deane relates a lovely tale of how the name came to be changed in 1914. M.E. Moore, a resident who attended school in Jackson, Mississippi, was being teased about being from a place called Dry Town, and so her father, O.P. Moore, successfully got the USPS to change the name to Mount Pleasant, with no hint of any barren dryness.

Mount Vernon (Faulkner): Established after the Civil War and briefly called Stonewall Jackson, then Housville or Houseville, because the post office was in the store of Tom House. The name was changed to Mount Vernon in 1877 to honor the first president.

Murfreesboro: The seat of Pike County was established as such in 1833 and originally called Zebulon. Deane is certain that this is in honor of Pike, but others are less sure, and it may well be biblical in origin. In 1836, the name was changed to Murfreesborough, allegedly because some of the early settlers came from that town in Tennessee. Deane recounts the admittedly silly but oft-told story of a traveler named Murphy who put down stakes here when his donkey died: Murphy's Burro.

Needmore (Scott): The story behind the odd name of this town, established in the 1920s, is that the owner of the local general store was perennially short of stock and would repeat, "I need more of that." It became a standing joke, and residents would keep asking for things in order to keep the joke going.

Negro Bend (Drew): A vanished town, probably founded by Blacks who had been run out of nearby Possum Valley by "white-caps."

Nellie's Apron (Baxter): In one of his best short essays, Deane tells two tales about a hired girl who worked at a boardinghouse used by railroad workers. In one story, she spots a broken rail on the line and uses her apron to flag down the train and avert disaster. In the other, a ne'er-do-well promises to come back for her but, of course, never does. Despondent, she wanders away, leaving only her apron hanging on a tree.

Nevada County *nuh-VAY-duh*: Formed in 1871 from parts of Columbia, Hempstead and Ouachita Counties. Received wisdom says it was so named because its shape resembled that of the state of Nevada, but perhaps the landowners were hopeful of valuable mineral deposits—or, at least, of luring settlers who had the same dreams.

Newark *NEW-ark* (Independence): This town was founded in 1882 when nearby Akron, which the White River had flooded repeatedly, moved to the line of a proposed railroad, and it was given its name by an unnamed landowner laying out the town. There are three guesses, none very persuasive, as to the origin of the name. First, the landowner proposed New Akron, but the citizens remaining in Akron objected; second, since the town was on high ground, it was regarded as a "new (biblical) ark"; or third, perhaps the name was just meant to indicate that this was a *new* town in *Ark*ansas.

New Hope (Drew): Settled in the mid-nineteenth century. After a tornado destroyed the church shortly after the Civil War, the town was rebuilt and named New Hope. What the original town name was and why are both unknown.

Newport: The current seat of Jackson County was established in the early nineteenth century as the site of a ferry crossing the White River and was called Tidwell's Landing. In the 1830s, the town became New Port, which soon elided into a single word. One story says that the "new" was to distinguish it from the "old port," Jacksonport, but since both towns were established around the same time, this seems unlikely. When the railroad was not welcomed in Jacksonport but came through Newport in 1872, most of the population of Jacksonport moved there. And with the demise of Jacksonport, Newport became the county seat in 1891.

North Little Rock (Pulaski): Established in 1838 as Huntersville, the town was laid waste by the Civil War. Later, the area was hopefully called Argenta, the Latin word for silver, on account of a nearby silver mine, and a neighborhood still retains the name. Deane notes that it was also at one time called DeCantillon, for an army officer who had dreamed of founding a city. When the railroad bridge was constructed across the Arkansas River in 1874, a project funded largely by two London brothers and financiers named Barling, the town was proclaimed Barling Cross. The confusion of real, honorary and folk names was resolved in 1917 when the town officially became North Little Rock.

Oark *OH-ark* (Johnson): When the town was settled in the nineteenth century, it was originally called Estep, almost certainly for a family. In 1879, the name was mysteriously changed to Oark, and local historians have long been puzzled about the rationale, with the prevalent and completely improbable explanation being that the name was easy to spell.

Oil Trough. *Courtesy of Joe Spake.*

Oil Trough (Independence): In the nineteenth century, black bears were a valued source of oil, used for lubrication, waterproofing, repelling mosquitoes and cooking, with a single bear providing several gallons of oil. A village on the White River, first known vaguely as Pleasant Island, was a center for bear hunters, many of whom would store their valuable oil in hollowed-out tree trunks. The better troughs could even be floated down the river for trade. The settlement, in 1849, was finally and officially named Oil Trough, probably for the hunting or possibly, as Deane suspects, because of all the wooden troughs left rotting along the river bank.

Old Joe (Baxter): One of the state's most interesting and controversial place names. When it was founded, the town was named for the neighboring mountain, called Old Naked Joe. There are at least four explanations for that name. One story tells of a "confused" man who used to run around in his altogether, while a second says that a tornado tore all the trees off Old Joe, which thereupon became Old Naked Joe. Deane located stories of hangings; one of a man who had lost his clothing, which may have been offensive but has seldom been a capital offense; and another of the hanging of an Indian named Old Joe, which seems a slim pretext for naming a mountain. Whatever the true story, when the town got its post office, the USPS insisted that the city drop "Naked" from its name.

Optimus (Stone): Settled in the 1880s, either the town was named for the Optimus tomato, a locally popular variety, or else the tomato was named for the town, either of which could be true and neither of which is supported by any evidence.

Pencil Bluff (Montgomery): Two communities, White Town and Sock City, agreed to combine in the 1940s, and one of the proponents of the union came up with this name. Probably this was owing to the appearance of a bluff, but the received story is that it commemorates the schoolchildren who, for many years, had written lessons on the slate slabs from the nearby bluffs.

Petit Jean River *PET-i JEEN*: A long river that runs into the Arkansas River near Petit Jean Mountain. An 1818 map drawn by Colonel Rene Paul calls the river the Little Yellow—or in French, Petit Jaune—but the stories that have grown up are far more interesting. Perhaps the oldest is the legend of the French maiden who dressed herself up like a cabin boy to follow her beloved and was nicknamed Little John or Petit Jean and immortalized by a lengthy poem. Another old story is that of a short Frenchman who was killed nearby. This story has picked up accretions, like the Frenchman being a soldier killed in a skirmish with Indians, with his corpse weighted and thrown into the river. Deane picked up the story of Jean la Caze, an aristocratic Frenchman fleeing the Revolution, whose wife and child died nearby. La Caze lost his mind, but his flute can still be heard.

Pickles Gap or **Pickle Gap** (Faulkner): There are two stories for this wonderful name. The first, rather mundanely but more probably, cites a local trapper named Piquell, while the second tells of a merchant fording the creek and upsetting his wagonload of pickles.

Plumerville *PLUHM-uhr-vil* (Conway): A stagecoach stop and later railroad depot was named for early landowner Samuel Plummer but lost an *m* along the way.

Pocahontas: The seat of Randolph County had been settled when the land was part of France and was called Encore de Fleuve Noir. When Randolph County was established, resident Ransom S. Bettis successfully had the town, which he called Bettis Bluff, named the county seat. But in 1837, the name was changed to that of the Native American woman, who in legend was an ancestor of John Randolph.

Portland (Ashley): Established in the 1850s as a steamboat landing on the Bayou Bartholomew and called "the port," it gradually took on its current name.

Princeton (Dallas): The longtime seat of Dallas County was, according to Deane, named either for the New Jersey City or for Albert Edward, Prince of Wales, when the town got its post office in 1845.

Promise Land (Ashley): According to local history, early settlers wrote eagerly to their families back in Mississippi that "they had found the Promise [*sic*] Land."

Push Mountain (Baxter): Deane says that the pass here was infamous for requiring anyone trying to get a team and wagon over it to get out and push.

Rabbit Ridge (Van Buren): Local history tells the tale of how, because of a farmer named Hare, the land was called Hare Hill, and this oddly (but neatly) evolved into Rabbit Ridge.

Republican (Faulkner): Originally called Cash Springs for early settler Gilbert Casharago, but the 1897 post office application for that name was refused. Local history says, improbably but possibly, that the town was thereupon named for the Republican administration.

Richmond (Little River): A typically implausible local tale says that it was settled after the Civil War and named for a "Mr. Richmond" who died while traveling through the area and is buried there.

Rob Hollow (Van Buren): The small town was, according to legend, so named because a small general store was robbed in the late nineteenth century but came out OK because the thief was unsuccessful in hiding the loot in the nearby valley and the money was recovered.

Rocky Comfort (Little River): Deane says that this town was first called Willow Springs, and he provides a thoroughly unbelievable tale of an "Indian chief" explaining that waters from the limestone springs provided a place for buffalo to drink in comfort.

Romance (White): When immigrants from Kentucky settled here prior to the Civil War, they called their settlement Kentucky Valley. According to local folklore, J.J. Walters, a local schoolteacher who thought the view from the bluffs was particularly romantic, renamed this tiny town around 1884.

As one might imagine, the Romance post office is extremely popular around Valentine's Day.

Rondo (Lee): Established around 1909 at a railroad intersection and named by early settler James S. Trigg, who did not explain the name. Some speculate that it derives from the French game of chance Rondeau. Records show that the first baby born after incorporation was named Rondo McKinney.

Rosie (Independence): When a town grew up in the early nineteenth century at a ferry, it was initially called White Run. In the 1880s, the postal service refused a request to rename the post office Edna, in honor of a daughter of the town founder. The second request had the word Rosie written in a margin, with no explanation; this was accepted and the town renamed.

Rule (Carroll): Deane recounts a cute if utterly incredible tale that the postmaster, needing to submit a name that was short and easy to spell, randomly snatched this word from an arithmetic textbook.

Saddle (Fulton): Ephraim Sharp founded the settlement in the 1870s. (This was the Ephraim Sharp of Fulton County, not to be confused with the Ephraim Sharp of Sharp County, although he was named for the Sharp County Sharp.) Anyway. The town was originally called Sharp's Mill, but the 1877 application for a post office called the settlement South Fork. In the 1950s, because of confusion with another South Fork, the USPS decreed that the town must change its name. The post office was located in a building with a general store in the front and Hershell Rogers's smithy in the back, and when word came of the need for another name, Ben Bishop was having a saddle repaired by Rogers. The men agreed to submit Saddle as a name, which was approved by the USPS.

St. James (Stone): Shave (or Shaved) Navel was the wonderful first name of this town, quickly followed by Buck Horn or Buckhorn in 1853, then St. James in 1883. One story says that Jesse James spent a night there en route to a robbery, staying with some residents related to the Youngers. This is a patently risible reason for the town's name, and a good story is desperately needed for the original one.

Sam's Throne (Newton): Deane tells a story about a local hunter, "Uncle" Sam Davis, who used to stand on a hill summit and preach about how someday he would sit on a throne, so the hilltop got the nickname.

Seaton Dump (Lonoke): This name absolutely requires a story, but none is yet known.

Selma (Drew): Settled in the mid-nineteenth century by Alabamians. When the railroad bypassed it, merchants moved their stores to Tillar but kept their homes here for the health benefits of living in the hills with fewer mosquitoes.

Sherwood (Pulaski): The farming community was first called Sylvan Hills in the late 1800s. When the town incorporated in 1948, it was renamed after the primary store in town, Sherwood Grocery.

The Skillet (Independence): Deane relates a cock-and-bull story of a fish fry during which the participants, three sheets to the wind, speculated about where on a cast-iron skillet they lived.

Smackover *SMAK-oh-vuhr* (Union): A 1789 letter from a French soldier refers to the Bayou de Chemin Couvert, meaning "covered way," and some consider this the origin of the name. Others point to a contemporary French description of the area as "covered with sumac," or *sumac couvert*, but Dickinson says "there is absolutely no foundation" for the sumac derivation. The first post office in 1879 was called Newport Landing, but its name changed the next year to Smackover. In 1890, residents moved about five miles south to where the railroad had been laid and businesses were springing up. The small town's population of ninety jumped to twenty-five thousand in 1922 when oil was discovered. Allsopp has a whole series of imaginary etymologies, most having to do with the town being "smack over" the creek. Deane rightly pooh-poohs anachronistic tales of oil gushing "smack over the derrick."

Sock City (Montgomery): Formed in the early twentieth century, with two stories for the name. One says that when they played poker, the locals used to hide their money in their socks. The second says that a nearby dance hall used to be the site of so many fights that the town got the name. Alas, it is now part of Pencil Bluff.

Spadra, creek, town and later New Spadra (Johnson): The site of an Indian trading factory in the early nineteenth century, where Spadra Creek empties into the Arkansas, it became an important riverboat landing. When, in the 1870s, the Little Rock & Fort Smith Railroad was persuaded to go through Clarksville instead of Spadra, many residents moved to the tracks and formed New Spadra. A town in California named Spadra was probably settled by someone from Arkansas. There is a cock-and-bull story, repeated by both Allsopp and Deane, about a Spanish explorer eloping with an Indian princess and fighting her family until his sword broke, with *spadra* being Spanish for "broken sword." Except that it isn't. Allsopp even provides names (Pedro, a soldier of de Soto, and Princess Coree) and a dreadful three-page-long poem about "The Broken Sword."

Spavinaw Creek (Benton): Deane relates a goofy story about a corruption of a French expression meaning "red shoots" or "young trees."

Spirit Lake (Lafayette): An oxbow lake formed when the Red River changed course and was named, says Deane, for sightings of the ghost of someone who drowned there.

Star City: The seat of Lincoln County was established in 1871, but the only stories for the name are unconvincing. One says that the five hills surrounding the site reminded someone of a star; another says that someone saw a falling star.

State Line (Lafayette): The obvious basis of this name is not so obvious, as the town is several miles from Louisiana.

Staves (Cleveland): Founded in the late nineteenth century and named for local mills that crafted staves for barrels and water lines. Also called Y for many years.

Staves. *Author's collection.*

Summit (Marion): When, in 1904, Jay Gould's railway bypassed Yellville and established a depot a few miles north of the town, most Yellville residents stubbornly chose not to relocate to the tracks. A new town eventually grew up around the depot and, being at a higher elevation than Yellville, naturally called itself Summit.

Sweet Home (Pulaski): This African American community, formed after the Civil War by former slaves turned small farmers, got its post office in 1877—named, according to Deane, for the Home Sweet Home Church. It was one of more than two dozen postbellum communities with this name but is the only one still extant.

Sylamore *SIL-uh-mor* (Izard): The town was built on Sylamore Creek and so called, according to local legend, for a reputed Indian horse thief, called "Chief Sylamore," who was finally tracked down and shot, and his body washed away in the creek. It seems likely that the creek is the only historically probable part of the tale, and the true origin of the name is now lost.

Temperanceville (Howard): A Methodist church was established in 1842, and a small community grew up around it, but there is no known explanation for this unusual name.

Texarkana *tex-ar-KAN-uh*: The sobriquet of the seat of Miller County, straddling the state line between Texas and Arkansas, also has a bit of thirty-mile-distant Louisiana's name thrown in for good measure. The name was allegedly the idea of a railroad surveyor, who nailed up a sign reading "Tex-Ark-Ana."

Tilly (Pope): A wonderful story says that in 1919, the first postmaster, Willie Dawkins, applied for the name Dahlonegah after his son, which the USPS dutifully rejected as too hard for anyone but Dawkins to spell. Dawkins, in frustration, picked a name from the comic strip *Tilly the Toiler*. Alas, the comic strip only went into syndication in 1921, so the origin of the name lies elsewhere.

Toad Suck (Faulkner): A nearly mythical ferry crossing on the Arkansas River. The story says it was so named because boatmen at a local tavern would suck on the bottle until they swelled up like toads. But Deane regretfully reports learning from a USGS researcher that a suck, like a

Toad Suck. *Courtesy of Mike Keckhaver.*

lick, was a place where animals would get water, and "toad" could refer to a narrow place in a stream, like the French *chute*, for channel—more likely, if less entertaining.

Tomato (Mississippi): First called Canadian Reach and then Cedar Landing when it was established in the late nineteenth century near the Mississippi. Floods forced the town to move, and it eventually vanished. There are two stories for the peculiar name. When determining the name for the post office, situated in the general store, a young girl pointed at a can of tomatoes and suggested that for the name. More colorfully, residents are said to have hung from a pole, or maybe a tree, a crate for riverboat deliveries. The crate had a bright tomato picture, so river captains began calling the site Tomato.

Tulip (Dallas): Settled in the 1830s. With two colleges, the town styled itself the Athens of the South, at least until the Civil War led to the town's demise. It was first called Brownsville and then Smithville, after local citizens. But local legend says that Colonel Maurice Smith urged changing the town's name to Tulip, because more tulip trees grew there than Smiths. Others claim that Presbyterians chose the name to honor the five Calvinist tenets. Deane reasonably suggests it's more likely that the name comes from the nearby Bayou de la Tulipe and the adjoining Cache de Tulipe, both probably named by a Frenchman named Tulipe.

Tulot (Poinsett): Deane says that the settlement was originally named Pickett, but this was too similar to nearby Piggott, so the name was changed to that of an Indian who used to live and hunt in the area. Allsopp says that

John Tulott was "an old Indian trapper" buried there, and the USPS lost track of one of the *t*'s.

Turkey Scratch (Phillips): The name of this now-vanished settlement—the boyhood home of musicians Robert Lockwood Jr. and Levon Helm—deserves a song, at least.

Twelve Corners (Benton): A town that grew in the 1850s around a Baptist church, most of the settlers having come from Twelve Corners, Tennessee.

Twin Groves (Faulkner): Formed in 1991 by a combining of two towns: Solomon's Grove (established by free Blacks from Memphis prior to the Civil War and named for one of the families) and Zion Grove, established around 1890, also by African Americans from Memphis.

Umpire (Howard): A wonderful name with a story that accrues more detail with each retelling. The basic tale involves a baseball game between local towns' teams, neither of which knew much about the game, and an authoritative umpire, whose judicial mien inspired the town's name. A 1973 history says that a local resident, perhaps schoolteacher "Miss Flora," made the suggestion to change the town name from Busby to Umpire. A history written by high school students nine years later says that the umpire was Billy Faulkner, cousin of Miss Flora. A 1988 history says that Faulkner was from Mena and the two teams were from Bethel and Galena, but the older legend says Galena was thumped by the team from Umpire.

Union County: Formed in 1829 and so named when the state legislature still felt that belonging to the American union was something worth celebrating.

Uno *YOO-noh* (Poinsett): A lumber camp was established in the early twentieth century, and when the residents were casting about for a name for the town, a respected citizen is said—however unlikely it seems—to have told the postmaster/storeowner, "You know, this is your store, and you can name it Uno."

Village (Columbia): Local history says, implausibly, that it was named for Village Creek, which was supposed to have been named by the Indians.

Vilonia (Faulkner): On early maps, the settlement was called Cypress Township, but when the Masonic lodge applied for a chapter in the 1860s, members proposed the name Vilsonia—signifying, according to somebody, "land of two valleys." The spelling "Vilonia" came back from the national office, and the community members simply let it stand to avoid all the red tape involved in correcting it.

Wabash (Phillips): Deane says that the town was settled early in the twentieth century and named by Indiana native S.E. Howe for the river that flowed through his hometown.

War Eagle, creek, mill and town (Benton): This famous site was allegedly named for an American Indian chief. Deane says that the town was settled in the 1830s along War Eagle Creek and cites "a historian and lawyer of the Cherokee nation" who suggested that this might be "an Osage sub-chief, Hurachis the War Eagle," known from some treaties of the 1820s. There's also a cock-and-bull story of a Cherokee brave named War Eagle dying along the creek after failing to find his beloved, who had been snatched by a White man.

Winchester (Drew): A depot established by the St. Louis, Iron Mountain and Southern Railroad near the plantation of John Martin Taylor, who had been born in Winchester, Kentucky. Taylor's plantation itself was called Hollywood.

Witts Springs (Searcy): An unlikely local tale says that the town was established in the 1870s and that a spring near the town had a stone with the word "Witts" engraved on it, so the town took that name.

Wye (Pulaski): A railroad "wye" allows an engine to turn around. Deane says that this wye served the Fourche River Lumber Co. and that the town was so named by C.H. Underwood, stationmaster and owner of a general store.

Yancopin *YAWN-kopin* (Desha): A small farming community grew up in the late nineteenth century where a railroad bridge over the Arkansas River was being constructed, and some residents remained since it was necessary for a worker to raise and lower the bridge to allow passage of large boats. The name comes from either a corruption of the Quapaw word for "water lily," *chinquapin*, or—a less likely but more interesting theory—because during the Civil War there was a stockade for captured Union troops, called a Yankee Pen.

Yardelle (Newton): Established in 1882 and originally called "the yard" or "the dell" for the work area of a prominent tanner and tombstone dresser and for the yarrow that grew there and had medicinal properties—which seems like a lot of stories for a very small town's name.

Y City (Scott): The settlement was named for the junction where Highway 270 splits off Highway 71.

BIBLIOGRAPHY

Research for this book involved dozens of county histories and journals of historical societies, as well as entries in the Central Arkansas Library System's *Encyclopedia of Arkansas*. Two newspapermen collected stories, and their books are foundational:

Allsopp, Fred W. *Folklore of Romantic Arkansas.* New York: Grolier Society, 1931.
Deane, Ernie. *Arkansas Place Names*. Branson, MO: Ozarks Mountaineer, 1986.

Most pronunciations were taken from:

Whaley, Storm. *They Call It: A Guide to the Pronunciations of Arkansas Place Names*. N.p.: Associated Press, 1950.

INDEX

Harkey Valley 40
Harrell 40
Harriet 40
Harrisburg 40
Harrison 40
Hartford 40
Hartman 86
Haskell 41
Hasty 134
Hatfield 86
Hattieville 99
Health 134
Heber Springs 41
Hector 134
Helena 41
Hempstead County 41
Hempwallace 86
Hensley 117
Herbine 135
Hickman 41
Hickory Ridge 67
Higden 99
Higginson 86
Highfill 41
Highland 67
Hillsboro 31
Hiwassee 86
Hogeye 135
Hogscald Hollow 135
Holland 41
Holly Grove 67
Hollywood 67
Holub 41
Hominy 135
Hon 42
Hookrum 136
Hope 86
Hopefield Lake 17
Hopper 99

Horatio 42
Horsehead Creek 136
Horseshoe Bend 67
Horseshoe Lake 67
Hot Spring County 67
Hot Springs 67
Howard County 42
Hoxie 86
Hugh 99
Hughes 42
Humnoke 136
Humphrey 86
Hunt 99
Hunter 42
Huntington 42
Huntsville 136
Huttig 42

I

Iceledo 136
Ico 136
Ida 99
Independence County 136
Indian Bay 136
Ink 136

J

Jackson County 23
Jacksonport 137
Jacksonville 86
Jamestown 42
Japton 43
Jasper 137
Jefferson County 23
Jenny Lind 43

Q

R

ABOUT THE AUTHOR

Dan Boice grew up in West Michigan and attended Calvin College in Grand Rapids. He received master's degrees in history and library science from the University of Michigan and has worked at academic libraries in Illinois, South Carolina, Iowa and Arkansas. He is currently the library director at the University of Arkansas at Monticello. With a dilettante's love for other languages, he especially enjoys the etymological riches of English and its regional variants.